Scripture and
Homosexuality

Scripture and Homosexuality

Biblical Authority and the Church Today

Marion L. Soards

Westminster John Knox Press
Louisville, Kentucky

Scripture quotations from the New Revised Standard Version of the Bible are copyright © 1989 by the Division of Christian Education of the National Council of the Churches of Christ in the U.S.A. and are used by permission.

Book design by Drew Stevens
Cover design by Tanya R. Hahn

First edition

Published by Westminster John Knox Press
Louisville, Kentucky

This book is printed on acid-free paper that meets the American National Standards Institute Z39.48 standard. ∞

PRINTED IN THE UNITED STATES OF AMERICA

95 96 97 98 99 00 01 02 03 04 — 10 9 8 7 6 5 4 3 2 1

Library of Congress Cataloging-in-Publication Data

Soards, Marion L., 1952-
    Scripture and homosexuality : biblical authority and the church today / Marion L. Soards. — 1st ed.
       p.   cm.
    ISBN 0-664-25595-7 (alk. paper)
    1. Homosexuality—Biblical teaching. 2. Homosexuality—Religious aspects—Christianity. I. Title
BS680.H67S64   1995
241'.66—dc20   95-2524

Contents

Preface

This book comes out of the ongoing process of study and discussion in the Presbyterian Church (U.S.A.) of human sexual behavior and orientation, especially regarding the ordination of homosexual persons. My involvement with this subject was initially not by choice. A little more than two years ago, the president of the seminary where I teach phoned me in behalf of himself and the president of the student body and asked me to speak at a monthly campus-wide forum on the topic "The Biblical Understanding of Homosexuality." I did not accept the invitation immediately; rather I asked for some time to think about it. Like most people these days I was busy—very busy. Besides, as C. S. Lewis once said, there are two kinds of speakers: Some agree to speak for the honor or the honorarium. Others speak, Lewis said, because they have something to say. There was certainly no honorarium for this talk, and I did not perceive much honor in the opportunity. When I was invited to speak on the biblical understanding of homosexuality, I did not feel compelled to talk about this topic publicly.

Like many other people, I had thought about the biblical understanding of homosexuality. In fact, because of

exegetical work I had done on key biblical passages, I
thought I saw where the real issues lay regarding the subject. Nevertheless, I had not thought through all the problems and evidence related to the topic. In one way, simply
reporting "the biblical understanding of homosexuality" is
easy, for the Bible says almost nothing about the matter,
and what is said is fairly easy to interpret if one has any exegetical training at all. Seeing clearly what the Bible says
about homosexuality is important, but a simple neutral
reading of the biblical texts does not finally answer the
question of what the church is to think and do about homosexuality today.

As I pondered the invitation to speak on the biblical
understanding of homosexuality, I recognized that agree-
ing to address this subject would ultimately force me to
draw some conclusions that went beyond where my thinking had previously led. I also knew that, should I grow
faint of heart, I could simply give a talk explaining the
Bible without ever having to say what I thought the biblical understanding of homosexuality means for Christians
today.

Like many members of the church, I have friends who
are lesbian or gay. These friends include people with
whom I was a student, former teachers and colleagues,
and students of my own from both earlier times and the
present. I must confess that because of my relationships
with these persons I tended to avoid thinking about the
Bible and homosexuality rather than to examine the matter
carefully. My own thinking in the past had been sloppy—
even incoherent—and it was rooted more in experience
than in theology. My own position, if one may call a set of
inconsistent thoughts a position, was to take an easy, per-
missive attitude toward homosexuality: Since we are all
sinners, it really does not matter whether homosexuality is

sinful, for God loves us all. And we ought to love one another rather than to argue about sexuality.

In turn, there were so many conflicting and strongly held convictions about homosexuality (most of them not well thought out) that I thought it imprudent to advocate policies about homosexuality. My private procedure, therefore, was to try to live without prejudices and to avoid controversies that are no-win situations. Prior to struggling with this topic, my opinion of both those who strongly opposed and those who strongly advocated acceptance of homosexuality was that they were hurting, not helping, the situation. Above all, as a biblical scholar I was tired of the irresponsible manner in which some on both sides of the debate used the Bible.

In the pages that follow, I have expanded my original reflections to consider the issues of biblical authority and interpretation, and I have examined the matters of Christian tradition, experience, and reason in relation to scripture in greater detail than I had in my earlier work. Finally, I have tried to reflect upon the meaning of scripture for the life of the church today as Christians seek to comprehend God's will regarding the matter of homosexuality. Nevertheless, there are times and topics in Christian thought and life that seem ambiguous, despite every effort to bring decisive evidence into view. Such matters demand informed discussion among the members of the community of faith.

This book is an attempt to contribute to that discussion. This study raises problems and produces implications, however, that I have not attempted to resolve or to pursue in these pages. I hope that what I have written helps as much to raise the necessary and appropriate questions for Christian reflection as to provide information and answers. I have, however, tried to make my own thinking on this subject clear, stating my own conclusions on various issues. I have learned from earlier publications on this topic that it is easy to be misunderstood. There was considerable reaction to my original paper on the biblical understanding of homosexuality. Several hundred letters came to me. Ninety-eight percent of them were hostile, and I was branded as everything from "an irresponsibly dangerous liberal iconoclast" to "an unmitigated fundamentalistic legalist." One critic, who completely misunderstood what I had written, wrote the president of our seminary imploring him to fire me before I could ruin a generation of prospective ministers. I can only ask that readers finish this book before they draw final conclusions about what I am saying.

I am grateful to my friend and editor, Dr. Davis Perkins, President and Publisher of Presbyterian Publishing Corporation, for inviting and persuading me to take on this project for Westminster John Knox Press. His concern to present a balanced publishing program to the church and to all those interested in this vital issue was what convinced me to undertake this work. What I have been able to learn in preparing this study has been gratifying, but I wish to confess in all honesty that the emotion and pain attached to the subject of this book have made this an exceedingly difficult project. Above all, I pray that this book will serve as a call for Christian candor and compassion, for until we learn as disciples of Christ to speak openly with one another in the spirit of Christ's own love, we will never grow or change or experience the gracious reconciliation that God intends for us as members of the one body of Jesus Christ.

Marion L. Soards
Advent 1994

1. Biblical Authority and the Reformed Tradition

At the heart of Christian faith is the *word* of God, God's self-revelation. As Christians we believe God's Word incarnate is Jesus Christ. We regard the Bible as God's written word, and we view Christian preaching as God's word proclaimed. The authority of God's Word is the foundation of the authority of the Bible. Indeed, the authority of the Bible resides in the subject to which it witnesses, not in the book itself.

Scripture in the Reformed Tradition

The authority of the Bible is a theological claim that cannot be logically demonstrated, but that rests in the conviction that God is uniquely related both to the origins of the scriptures in the past and to the use of the scriptures now. The Bible has authority because the Holy Spirit takes human witnesses and, through their witness, brings about faith and obedience to Jesus Christ. We ourselves recognize the authority of the Bible "in dependence on the illumination of the Holy Spirit" (The Confession of 1967, 9.30).

We can and must distinguish between the Bible as the

word of God and Jesus Christ as God's Word, between God in our midst and a book about God's will and work. Yet we should see that there is a solidarity between Jesus Christ and the Bible; for we know the incarnate and personal Word of God only as we encounter him in and through the written word of God. Thus the Reformed tradition has held and maintains a high view of scripture, so that we in the Presbyterian Church (U.S.A.) read in *The Book of Confessions:*

> As we believe and confess the Scriptures of God sufficient to instruct and make perfect the man of God, so do we affirm and avow their authority to be from God, and not to depend on men or angels. We affirm, therefore, that those who say the Scriptures have no other authority save that which they have received from the [church] are blasphemous against God and injurious to the true [church], which always hears and obeys the voice of her own Spouse and Pastor, but takes not upon her to be mistress over the same (The Scots Confession, 3.19).

> CANONICAL SCRIPTURE. We believe and confess the canonical Scriptures of the holy prophets and apostles of both Testaments to be the true Word of God, and to have sufficient authority of themselves, not of men. For God himself spoke to the fathers, prophets, apostles, and still speaks to us through the Holy Scriptures.

> And in this Holy Scripture, the universal Church of Christ has the most complete exposition of all that pertains to a saving faith, and also to the framing of a life acceptable to God; and in this respect it is expressly commanded by God that nothing be either added to or taken from the same.

> SCRIPTURE TEACHES FULLY ALL GODLINESS. We judge, therefore, that from these Scriptures are to be derived true wisdom and godliness, the reformation and government of the churches; as also instruction in all duties of piety; and, to be short, the confirmation of doctrines,

and the rejection of all errors, moreover, all exhortations according to that word of the apostle, 'All Scripture is inspired by God and profitable for teaching, for reproof,' etc. (II Tim. 3:16–17) (The Second Helvetic Confession, 5.001-5.003a).

Under the name of Holy Scripture, or the Word of God written, are now contained all the books of the Old and New Testaments. . . . All which are given by inspiration of God, to be the rule of faith and life (The Westminster Confession of Faith, 6.002).

The whole counsel of God, concerning all things necessary for his own glory, man's salvation, faith, and life, is either expressly set down in Scripture, or by good and necessary consequence may be deduced from Scripture: unto which nothing at any time is to be added, whether by new revelations or the Spirit, or traditions of men. Nevertheless we acknowledge the inward illumination of the Spirit of God to be necessary for the saving understanding of such things as are revealed in the Word; and that there are some circumstances concerning the worship of God, and the government of the Church, common to human actions and societies, which are to be ordered by the light of nature and Christian prudence, according to the general rules of the Word, which are always to be observed (The Westminster Confession of Faith, 6.006).

The Supreme Judge, by which all controversies of religion are to be determined, and all decrees of councils, opinions of ancient writers, doctrines of men, and private spirits, are to be examined, and in whose sentences we are to rest, can be no other but the Holy Spirit speaking in the Scripture (The Westminster Confession of Faith, 6.010).

Q.3. What do the Scriptures principally teach?
A. The Scriptures principally teach what man is to believe concerning God, and what duty God requires of man (The Shorter Catechism, 7.003).

Q.3. What is the Word of God?

A. The holy Scriptures of the Old and New Testaments are the Word of God, the only rule of faith and obedience.

Q.4. How doth it appear that the Scriptures are the Word of God?

A. The Scriptures manifest themselves to be the Word of God, by their majesty and purity; by the consent of all the parts, and the scope of the whole, which is to give all glory to God; by their light and power to convince and convert sinners, to comfort and build up believers unto salvation. But the Spirit of God, bearing witness by and with the Scriptures in the heart of man, is alone able fully to persuade it that they are the very word of God.

Q.5. What do the Scriptures principally teach?

A. The Scriptures principally teach, what man is to believe concerning God, and what duty God requires of man (The Larger Catechism, 7.113-7.115).

The one sufficient revelation of God is Jesus Christ, the Word of God incarnate, to whom the Holy Spirit bears unique and authoritative witness through the Holy Scriptures, which are received and obeyed as the word of God written. The Scriptures are not a witness among others, but the witness without parallel. The church has received the books of the Old and New Testaments as prophetic and apostolic testimony in which it hears the word of God and by which its faith and obedience are nourished and regulated (The Confession of 1967, 9.27).

We trust in God the Holy Spirit . . . the same Spirit who inspired the prophets and apostles [and] rules our faith and life in Christ through Scripture (A Brief Statement of Faith, 10.4).

Yet despite our regularly spoken concern with the Bible, there is abundant evidence that we may not mean what we say.

1. Recently, a biblical scholar was asked to speak at a major Bible conference in the eastern United States. The setting was an evening event in a large pavilion where several hundred people gathered for Bible study in the context of a worship service. About five minutes before the session was to begin, several of the worship leaders were scurrying among the people speaking with one group after another. Shortly thereafter the main liturgist sheepishly approached the speaker and said, "It's time to start but we can't find a Bible to read the scripture lesson. Do you have one we could use?" The speaker had only a Greek New Testament, which proved unhelpful for the liturgist. So the assembly spent twenty minutes singing while someone drove to the nearest church to bring back a copy of an English Bible. It may have been a sheer anomaly, but at least once, people did not even bother to bring their Bibles to a Bible conference.

2. At the level of the most basic information we have difficulties with the Bible: (a) A roomful of high school Sunday school students was asked, How many disciples did Jesus have? Only one boy knew; but when asked to name them he could come up only with Peter and Paul. (b) Even seminarians and pastors lack primary facts. A small minority of such persons tested could answer the following four questions accurately: (i) How many books are in the Bible? Sixty-six. (ii) How many books are in the New Testament? Twenty-seven. (iii) Who is *the* major New Testament author? Luke, the author of Luke and Acts. Even the thirteen letters attributed to Paul in the New Testament amount to less material than that found in Luke and Acts. (iv) In which Testament is the book of Hezekiah? Neither. The person Hezekiah is in the Old Testament, but there is no book called by that name.

While mastering biblical facts does not guarantee a

concern with the Bible as authoritative testimony to God's work for salvation, a high view of the Bible normally results in serious study of its writings. Yet the evidence seems to indicate, despite our stated position, that we lack concern for the Bible or that we do not take the Bible seriously.

A pragmatic argument only illustrates—it does not establish—the authority of scripture, but time and again, Christians—through involvement with the Bible—have found themselves judged, called, and compelled to an essentially Christian faith and life. We need only recall Augustine, the Reformers, Martin Luther King Jr., and Mother Teresa to underscore the point.

This formation and transformation of life through engagement with scripture occurs because of four charcteristics of the Bible. It is

1. *Vital.* The scriptures stand in proximity to the original events that formed the church. They testify to God's work among Israel, and especially to the life, death, resurrection, and exaltation of Jesus Christ. The Bible bears witness to God's formative activity amid the people of Israel and the earliest Christians.

2. *Discerning.* In its articulation of Israel's and early Christianity's beliefs and practices, the Bible testifies to the profundity of Jewish and Christian perception and reflection on God's revelation.

3. *Trustworthy.* The scriptures were written as information about experiences, beliefs, and practices in order to provide guidance; and subsequent generations of believers have proved the Bible's usefulness over and over.

4. *Normative.* Above all, the scriptures provide us with a norm or a means to judge between the spirits. The Bible guides us as we seek faithfully to decide among the competitive claims that arise in the life of the church. It is "the witness without parallel" (The Confession of 1967, 9.27).

The Necessity of Interpretation

We must recognize that using the Bible as the authoritative source for the belief and practice of the church is not without its difficulties. The Bible was written long ago and far away: (1) in different times—from more than a thousand years before Christ to several decades after his death; (2) in different places—the Mediterranean and the Near East; (3) in different cultures—Semitic and Greco-Roman; (4) in different languages—Hebrew, Aramaic, and Greek, with reference to and evidence of the influence of Latin.

We cannot ignore these and many other factors as we turn to read the Bible. Frankly, they form barriers, and we need help in reading with real understanding because all reading of the Bible requires interpretation of the texts.

In fact, all reading of the Bible *is* interpretation. We frequently make automatic distinctions as we read; for example, we distinguish between poetic and nonpoetic elements in the biblical texts. Thus, when the Elder addresses his audience in 1 John as "little children," we do not conclude that his remarks were aimed at an assembly of infants and youths. But when the Gospels tell us that Jesus went to Capernaum—unless we are ardent devotees of wild allegorization—we conclude that Jesus went to a particular geographical location. When the Genesis story tells us that "Esau is a hairy man," we do not expect to gain much spiritual edification from the information.

In turn, we automatically do interpretation based on these distinctions. "The Lord is my shepherd" is not information about divine animal husbandry; nor is it a claim by the psalmist to be a sheep. Psalm 23 is a profound statement of faith about God's care for humanity and about the security of the believer, or as Calvin would put it, about "sovereignty" and "perseverance of the saints."

Similarly, "Behold the Lamb of God" (John 1:29, 36) is not John the Baptist's mistaking Jesus for a sheep. It is a christological confession that recognizes "Jesus is the paschal Lamb of the Christian Passover who by his death (at the very moment the paschal lambs were being killed in the Temple) delivered the world from sin, as the original paschal lamb's blood delivered the Israelites from the destroying angel" (R. E. Brown, *The Gospel and Epistles of John: A Concise Commentary* [4th ed.; Collegeville, Minn.: Liturgical Press, 1988], 25).

In instances such as these, the necessity and practice of interpretation occur naturally. But sometimes in reading scripture we do not automatically make distinctions, and therefore we do not do interpretation (correctly), and so we misunderstand. For example, in John 3 Jesus tells Nicodemus that he must be born *anōthen*. Here *anōthen* is an ambiguous Greek word that can mean "again" or "from above," and Nicodemus hears "again" rather than "from above," so that his subsequent remarks are at least as comical as they are tragic. Jesus declares that humans must be born "from above"—that is, by the power of God renewing their lives. Humans need to be "born anew," but in the sense of rebirth by God's power at work in their lives rather than merely being born "once more." Unfortunately, Nicodemus is not the only one who fails to grasp Jesus' meaning, for many in the world today cheerfully use the language of Nicodemus's misunderstanding to describe their theological conviction that they are "born again."

Similarly, in John 12:32 Jesus said, "And I, when I am lifted up from the earth, will draw all people to myself"; and the reader is forced to ask, What does "being lifted up" mean? Does it refer to crucifixion, to exaltation, or to both? Careful study of the word *hypsoō*, "lifted up" in this passage, or even careful study of the larger speech in which Jesus makes this statement, probably will not provide a final answer to this question; for, in context, the statement functions as a prophecy of Jesus' death. Yet in the broader range of John's theological reflection as it is known from the entire Gospel, it is the crucified and exalted Lord who (through the Spirit) draws humanity to himself.

This observation about John 12:32 leads to a larger issue regarding the Bible: At its very heart, the Bible records and communicates information that requires interpretation in order that the information have relevance for faith and life. Indeed, it is in the process of interpretation that the biblical information becomes relevant. Moreover, the Bible itself bears witness to the necessity of our interpreting its message because the biblical authors themselves engage in theological interpretation.

Consider, for example, the death of Jesus: On the surface, as a mere fact, Jesus' death is but a tragic ending to the life of a seemingly good but probably imprudent first-century Jew. But through Jesus' own teaching and the disciples' experience of the resurrection of Jesus, the early church knew Jesus' death to be more than a fact of history. Therefore, the New Testament never really speaks of Jesus' death at its sheerly historical level but always in and through interpretation. Indeed, that the church's interpretation of Jesus' death did not occur simply "once upon a time," that in the light of the resurrection the earliest believers struggled to grasp the depths of the meaning of Christ's death—both are clear from the wealth of images recorded in the New Testament offering interpretation of Jesus' death.

Consider only Paul: For him (and other early Christians) Jesus' death was the fulfillment of scriptures; thus

Jesus' death was described and explained in scriptural terms (Old Testament) as an expiatory sacrifice (1 Cor. 5:7; Rom. 3:25—see Lev. 16:13–15; Ex. 12:21–27); as divine humiliation in obedience (Phil. 2:6–11—see Isa. 53:3, 11; 45:22–23); as divine redemption on the model of buying out of consecrated service into freedom (1 Cor. 6:20; 7:23—see Lev. 27:1–21); and as rescue on the models of the Exodus or the appeals of the Psalms for deliverance from peril (Rom. 7:24; 2 Cor. 1:10; 1 Thess. 1:10—see, for example, Ex. 5:23; 6:6; 12:27; 14:30; Pss. 6:4; 7:1; 17:13; 18:17; 56:13).

All these images are metaphors for expressing the crucial conviction that *Jesus' death brings salvation!* Thus, we see that Paul declares the saving significance of Jesus' death in the language of Old Testament salvific motifs.

The Bible itself informs us that early Christians turned to the scriptures in order to comprehend in greater depth the meaning of God's saving work in Jesus Christ. With the Bible as our model, we ourselves must engage in study and interpretation of the scriptures that they may speak anew to us as they spoke to those first Christians. We must come to know what it means to confess that "Christ died for our sins in accordance with the scriptures . . . and that he was raised on the third day in accordance with the scriptures" (1 Cor. 15:3–4).

Christ Our Hermeneutic

What, then, is the basis of our interpretation? How shall we go about this crucial work? Three concerns coalesce:

1. What the Bible says to each of us as individuals.
2. What the Bible has said to those before us and with us in the life of the church.
3. What the biblical writings said to their first readers,

or what we perceive the author intended to say to the original audience.

These are all valid questions (though the answers are debatable), but a key for accurate interpretation is the sequence of our posing these questions.

I would argue that our primary task as interpreters is to ask (3); it is only when we have resolved this issue that we are in a position to ask and then critique (2) and (1). Interpreting in this manner is not to deny that the Bible can speak in distinct ways in different times and places; but to determine the validity of what I or you or our predecessors in faith conclude the Bible means, we must ask whether our interpretations are congruent with the "plain sense" of the scriptures. In order to control, to guide, to criticize, and to guarantee appropriate interpretation, we must become informed and active readers. We must educate ourselves in terms of history, ancient philosophy and religion, languages, theology, and hermeneutics. This strategy for reading scripture does not mean that Christians who are not biblical scholars are unable to read the Bible with perception and insight. Yet the distance between ourselves and the Bible and the long history of interpretation—with explanations that sometimes conflict or contradict each other—means that scholars have a responsibility to contribute to the study of the scriptures in the life of the church.

The interpretive elements of history, philosophy and religion, languages, and theology are fairly straightforward, although they imply a high degree of sophistication for the interpreter; but because of its complexity the following paragraphs focus on hermeneutics. Simply defined, *hermeneutics* designates the methods, the means, and the measure of our interpretations.

What is the standard of our interpretation of scripture? Some propose justice, others liberation, still others love— all noble standards—but I would insist that the criterion for our understanding of the Bible is *Jesus Christ himself*. "The one sufficient revelation of God is Jesus Christ, the Word of God incarnate"(The Confession of 1967, 9.27); and "the Bible is to be interpreted in the light of its witness to God's work of reconciliation in [Jesus] Christ" (The Confession of 1967, 9.29).

If we confess Jesus Christ to be the incarnate Word of God, then we must hold him at the beginning and at the center of our faith. The distinctive character of Christianity is that it focuses on God and the relationship between God and humanity (and, for that matter, the cosmos) by focusing on the person of Jesus Christ and the personal relationship with Jesus Christ that humanity and creation enjoy.

Interpretation of scripture is an encounter with a text, not with a person. But because we know the person of Jesus Christ as he is mediated to us through the scriptures, no interpretation of the Bible can be called Christian that is devoid of the inherently personal quality of Christian faith. In one way, an honest atheist can do valid historical interpretation of the Bible, but in the context of the community of faith we should strive to effect a personal quality in our historical interpretation.

At a stark minimum our work in interpreting the Bible should be a three-way encounter: between the texts, ourselves, and the personal presence of our risen Lord, all "under the guidance of the Holy Spirit" (The Confession of 1967, 9.29). Further, an awareness of the presence of Christ in our lives—in the work of interpreting scripture—should immediately remind us that we are not on an individualistic journey, where we as individuals (or cliques), along with Jesus Christ and the Bible, "have a good thing going."

Perhaps the best image for what it means to do valid interpretation is that of an open roundtable discussion. We can imagine the Bible (even its authors) at table with us, with Jesus Christ, and with representatives of the community of faith. The Bible is neither "mine" nor "ours" alone—it is the scripture of the church universal; it is the most basic testimony to our Lord and God. Thus we invite Christ's people to our conversation.

By necessity, a significant number of those at the interpretive table will be scholars and prominent leaders of the church who have long read and interpreted the Bible. But the church is more than a brain or a mouth. The body of Christ comprises eyes, ears, hands, feet, and heart. Thus, in attempting to hear the voice of scripture—or the voices of the Bible—we must carefully call for the insights of all Christ's people, not merely those most compatible with our points of view.

As we work with scripture, we must understand that in the overall process of interpretation, we ourselves—our very persons and lives—are being called into question. The labor of interpreting the Bible does not necessarily lead to a comforting confirmation of who we are and what we do. No interpretation of the Bible is truly valid wherein the interpreters are not as vulnerable as the text. We encounter the Bible in the context of the total community of faith, and we, others, and the scriptures are all together under the Lordship of Jesus Christ. In the give and take of interpretation we must constantly hold the interpretations of all partners in the conversation up against the person of Christ, who is the final criterion for valid understanding.

Jesus means freedom. The call of Christ is a call to freedom, to liberation from all involvements that enslave us and others, and thereby reduce our lives to levels less than that intended by God in creation and redemption. Moreover, we are freed not only *from* oppression but *for* a rich, rewarding relationship to Christ that means a life of loving service to others according to Christ's will. The interpretation of the Bible must be done in the context of these concerns and commitments. Interpretation must always raise the Christ-centered questions of liberation and obligation, of freedom and service.

We find our way forward, as God would have us go, when we read the Bible and attend to its message as illuminated by the Holy Spirit. Without the gifts of the word of God written and the guidance of the Spirit we are left to our own devices, and as Calvin said, "The whole world lies in wickedness" and the mind of this world is "a false imagination" (*Commentaries on the Epistle of Paul the Apostle to the Romans* [Grand Rapids: Wm. B. Eerdmans, 1959], 453–55). Against that negative situation, however, our God who reconciles us in Jesus Christ gives us scripture and the Spirit to direct us in our faithfulness.

2. The Biblical Understanding of Homosexuality

The Bible says remarkably little about homosexuality. In fact, there is no biblical word for homosexual or for homosexuality. The relevant texts tend to speak graphically about actions, not about persons or sexual orientations. Indeed, some of the biblical passages that are regularly invoked in debates about homosexuality prove upon examination to have little or nothing to do with the subject.

Pertinent Old Testament Texts

For example, the well-known story in Genesis 19 about Sodom and Gomorrah and the lesser-known (parallel?) account in Judges 19 about Gibeah are concerned with gang-rape violence and flagrant disregard for the sacred obligation to provide hospitality. The depravity of the characters in these stories is not simply equivalent with homosexuality. The villainous men in these stories certainly desired and intended to commit homosexual acts, and their intentions are regarded by the narrators of the accounts as being ignoble and immoral. But in the biblically formed mind as we know it from subsequent biblical texts,

Sodom and Gomorrah became symbols of God's judgment, not symbols of homosexuality (see, e.g., Deut. 29:23; Isa. 1:9–10; Jer. 23:14; 49:18; 50:40; Lam. 4:6; etc.).

Ezekiel 16:49 says, "This was the guilt of your sister Sodom: she and her daughters had pride, excess of food, and prosperous ease, but did not aid the poor and needy." This pattern of remembering Sodom and Gomorrah as symbols of God's judgment appears in the New Testament in Matthew (10:15; 11:23–24), Mark (6:11), Luke (10:12; 17:29), Romans (9:29), 2 Peter (2:6), Jude (v. 7), and perhaps Revelation (11:8). The stories and references to Sodom and Gomorrah say little or nothing about our subject.

Leviticus, however, contains two texts that are more pertinent to our concern. First, Lev. 18:22 reads, "You shall not lie with a male as with a woman; it is an abomination." Second, Lev. 20:13 declares, more severely, "If a man lies with a male as with a woman, both of them have committed an abomination; they shall be put to death; their blood is upon them."

Both these verses are parts of the ⁴Holiness Code of Israel, a set of regulations for the lifestyle of the Israelites that was meant to distinguish the Israelites from their neighbors by directing the life of the Hebrew people and their religious practices as they lived among foreign nations and foreign religions. We must recognize that along with proscriptions against homosexual activities, the Holiness Code of Leviticus 17–26 contains prohibitions against eating rare meat; against incest; against bestiality; against harvesting all the grain in a field or all the grapes in a vineyard; against stealing, lying, and cheating; against wearing clothes made of two different materials; against trimming one's forelocks; against shaving; and against wearing tattoos, among other things. Thus the Holiness Code clearly contains a combination of purity regulations and moral prescriptions, and the church in the power of the Spirit has elected to preserve some of these laws and to set aside others; thus a statement made in Leviticus does not automatically apply to Christians.

Given the historical setting and purpose of the Holiness Code in which Lev. 18:22 and 20:13 occur, and more, given that we confess in faith that Christ is the end of the law (Rom. 10:4), it is impossible to declare the necessary relevance of these verses for our world today. Should some object to this observation, let them remember that in Galatians Paul says mockingly, "For all who rely on the works of the law are under a curse; for it is written, 'Cursed is everyone who does not observe and obey all the things written in the book of the law'"; and later he writes, "Once again I testify to every man who lets himself be circumcised that he is obliged to obey the entire law. You who want to be justified by the law have cut yourselves off from Christ; you have fallen away from grace" (Gal. 3:10–11; 5:3–4). Grace, not law, governs Christian life. •

Moreover, on the one hand Calvin recognized "the third use of the Law" for "believers in whose hearts the Spirit of God already flourishes and reigns" as "the best instrument for enabling them daily to learn with greater truth and certainty what that will of the Lord is which they aspire to follow, and to confirm them in this knowledge" (*Inst.* 2.7.12). On the other hand he recognized that "the case of ceremonies is different, these having been abrogated not in effect but in use only . . . for as these ceremonies would have given nothing to God's ancient people but empty show, if the power of Christ's death and resurrection had not been prefigured in them . . . it would, in the present day, be impossible to understand for what purpose they were insti-

tuted" (*Inst.* 2.7.16). Thus we must ask whether the New
Testament text has similar statements or remarks that
would indicate that the earliest Christians preserved particular elements of the Levitical Holiness Code as valid in-
structions for Christian thought and life.

New Testament References
to Homosexuality

With regard to homosexuality, three passages from the
New Testament demand consideration: Rom. 1:26–27; 1
Cor. 6:9; and 1 Tim. 1:10. Because of the similar language
and similar function in context of 1 Cor. 6:9 and 1 Tim. 1:10,
and because of the distinctively weighty nature of Rom.
1:26–27, I shall consider 1 Corinthians and 1 Timothy together before turning to Romans.

In 1 Cor. 6:9–11 Paul chides the Corinthians for their
spiritual arrogance that led to their failure to address im-
morality and intrachurch disputes in a responsible fashion.
In exhorting the Corinthians to faithful action Paul contrasts their present quality of life in Christ with their past
unrighteousness. To make his point Paul catalogues in
stereotypical fashion the previous unrighteous characteris-
tics of the now-justified Corinthians. He describes those
who belong to this world, not God's kingdom, in this way:
"Do not be deceived! Fornicators, idolaters, adulterers,
male prostitutes, sodomites, thieves, the greedy, drunk-
ards, revilers, robbers—none of these will inherit the kingdom of God. And this is what some of you used to be."

The word translated in the NRSV as "male prostitutes"
is *malakoi* in Greek and means literally "soft ones," probably referring to the so-called passive partner in homosexual activity. The word translated as "sodomites" is

arsenokoitai, literally, "male bedders," perhaps referring to the "other" partner in the homosexual arrangement. These words have sorely vexed interpreters and translators.

The influential work of John Boswell, *Christianity, Social Tolerance, and Homosexuality* (Chicago/London: University of Chicago Press, 1980), argued vigorously that *malakoi* indicated "unrestrained" or "wanton" or "dissolute," and *arsenokoitai* indicated "male prostitutes." Thus one sometimes reads or hears that there is no denunciation of homosexual activity in 1 Corinthians 6. Because of the incisive work of Robin Scroggs in *The New Testament and Homosexuality* (Philadelphia: Fortress, 1983), however, interpreters almost universally understand the word *arsenokoitai* in 1 Cor. 6:9 to be an idiom derived from the Septuagintal version of Lev. 18:22, which in part reads *kai meta arsenos ou koimēthēsē koitēn gynaikos* ("and you shall not sleep in bed with a man as with a woman"), and of Lev. 20:13, which contains the words *kai hos an koimēthē meta arsenos koitēn gynaikos* ("and whoever may lie in bed with a man as with a woman"). Thus Paul's declaration presupposes the condemnation of homosexual acts by the Holiness Code of Leviticus. Similarly, 1 Tim. 1:9 discusses the value of the law (i.e., the legal portions of the Jewish scriptures) for "the lawless and disobedient." Then, 1 Tim. 1:9–10 contains a list illustrating who are lawless and disobedient. The list includes the word *arsenokoitai* ("male bedders") again, apparently assuming Lev. 18:22 and 20:13, or at least 1 Cor. 6:9.

Both of these statements occur in the situational remarks of the epistles. The author is busy arguing against a concrete problem in the life of the church, not homosexuality itself, and simply mentions homosexual activity along with other unacceptable activities in an effort to illustrate the central point of the argument. Thus the remarks have more rhetorical force than regulatory value. In other words, at the point that we find 1 Cor. 6:9 and 1 Tim. 1:10, the letters are not doing constructive theological reflection. Both these verses illustrate unacceptable behavior: pre-Christian practices in 1 Corinthians and actions "contrary to the sound teaching that conforms to the glorious gospel of the blessed God" in 1 Timothy. The primary intention of these verses is not to teach about homosexuality, and only indirectly may we derive information regarding homosexuality from this material.

Paul's Theological Reflections in Romans

The case is different when we come to Romans. Paul's explicit statements concerning both male and female homosexuality in Rom. 1:26–27 are made in the course of serious and significant theological reflection. Paul states his major theme in Rom. 1:16–17, "For I am not ashamed of the gospel; it is the power of God for salvation to everyone who has faith, to the Jew first and also to the Greek. For in it the righteousness of God is revealed through faith for faith, as it is written, 'The one who is righteous will live by faith.'" Then in Rom. 1:18–3:20 Paul carefully crafts an argument designed to make the point stated in 3:9, "All, both Jews and Greeks, are under the power of sin." The point is reiterated in 3:23, "All have sinned and fall short of the glory of God."

Paul's chief concern is to declare that God's righteousness means the salvation of all humankind as God works to create saving faith in an otherwise sinful humanity. But in order to make clear to the Roman readers how great a work God's salvation is, Paul discusses the hopeless sinful condition of humanity. First, in 1:18–32 Paul turns toward the Gentiles, discussing their fundamental sin of idolatry. Second, having declared the failure of the Gentiles to acknowledge and honor God, Paul turns toward the Jews and declares them equally guilty because they trusted and revered the law rather than God. Both Gentiles and Jews have ignored the one true God as they trusted idols or the law and their own human devices. In ignoring God and trusting something less than God both Gentiles and Jews (i.e., all humanity) sin against God.

As Paul discusses the Gentile sin of idolatry, he refers to their homosexual behavior as the clear symptom of their sinfulness. Note well: homosexuality is not the Gentiles' problem, it is a *symptom* of their problem. They are under the power of sin, and they are isolated from God. Writing about this passage, Richard Hays remarks,

> Paul singles out homosexual intercourse for special attention because he regards it as providing a particularly graphic image of the way in which human fallenness distorts God's created order. God the creator made man and woman for each other, to cleave together, to be fruitful and multiply. When human beings engage in homosexual activity, they enact an outward and visible sign of an inward and spiritual reality: the rejection of the Creator's design. They *embody* the spiritual condition of those who have "exchanged the truth about God for a lie" (*Sojourners* 20 [July 1991]: 19).

Listen to Paul in vv. 25–27: "Because they exchanged the truth about God for a lie and worshiped and served the creature rather than the Creator, . . . for this reason God gave them up to degrading passions . . . [they] received in their own persons the due penalty for their error."

According to Paul, homosexual activity is not a sin that provokes God's wrath; rather, the wrath of God comes on humans who are under the power of sin. A sign of both God's wrath and human sin is that humans engage in homosexual acts.

One approach to this passage that tries to tone down the negative assessment of homosexuality suggests that Paul is not denouncing those who are truly homosexual. Rather, it is argued that Paul is referring to licentious heterosexual persons who have engaged in homosexual acts. The text says that "their women exchanged natural intercourse for unnatural" and that the men gave up "natural intercourse with women" and "were consumed with passion for one another." Paul, however, is not concerned with individual decisions. He is discussing the sinful guilt of all humans; moreover, neither Paul nor any other ancient person had a concept of "sexual orientation." For Paul and Jewish thinkers such as Philo and Josephus, as well as first-century Greco-Roman moralists such as Seneca, Plutarch, and Dio Chrysostom, homosexual acts were willful actions of unbridled lust.

Paul's argument in Romans would be very persuasive for those to whom he wrote. His readers were familiar with similar denunciations from both Jewish and non-Jewish thinkers of the Hellenistic period. But remember, Paul's real criticism is aimed at Gentile idolatry. Paul states that God's wrath toward this Gentile sin is graphically evident in God's giving up the Gentiles to homosexual activity. As soon as Paul's readers agree with his point, he tells them in Rom. 2:1, "Therefore you have no excuse, whoever you are, when you judge others; for in passing judgment on another, you condemn yourself because you, the judge, are doing the very same things." To summarize Paul's main argument: All humans are under the power of sin; no one sin or sinner is better off than another; God's grace freely redeems all humankind through the faith of Jesus Christ.

The Findings from Scripture

What then have we found? Portions of the New Testament indicate that the early Christians accepted as valid the denunciations of homosexual activity in the Levitical Holiness Code. The one statement in the New Testament that treats homosexuality in the context of a deliberate theological reflection is Rom. 1:26–27. There Paul assesses the sinful condition of all humans. He works from the beliefs and traditions of his own time to articulate a theological vision of reality by which the Roman readers and other early Christians are to gain their theological bearings for life. God's purpose for humanity, as Paul and the others knew it from created order, scripture, and perhaps the words of Jesus, was for man and woman, male and female, to find fulfillment in the complementary sexual union that God intended in the creation.

Paul was not concerned with the origins, motivations, or gratifications of homosexual activity, nor were other ancient thinkers interested in these issues. Arguments about the genetic or sociological origins of homosexuality, about the phenomenon of mutual consent between adult homosexual partners, about genuinely loving homosexual relationships—none of these would impress Paul. He would simply understand the use of such information in arguments for the acceptance of homosexual behavior as further evidence of the blindness of humanity in bondage to sin.

As Paul discerned and declared God's relationship to humans, homosexual acts were outside the boundaries of

God's intentions for humanity. Homosexuality was one vivid indication of the real problem of sin, and Paul states bluntly that all humans are sinners. On the matter of homosexuality, we should see clearly that the biblical understanding of homosexual behavior is univocal (although this issue is at most a minor concern). Homosexual activity is not consistent with the will of God; it is not merely a sin but evidence of sin, and there is no way to read the Bible as condoning homosexual acts.

The Church's Responsibility

So what finally do we make of this finding? Modern Christians have multiple sources of authority to which they turn for sorting out life's complex and controversial issues.

1. There is science. The evidence, however, is mixed. Is homosexual orientation genetically determined, socially conditioned, or both? Perhaps homosexuality should not be regarded as a monolithic phenomenon. What are we to make of the claims of sexual reorientation? Can one alter a sexual orientation from homosexual to heterosexual behavior? Can all do so?

2. There is experience. Here too the evidence is mixed. There are more and less noble forms of homosexual activity, though even decent, loving homosexual couples are no validation of the appropriateness of homosexual behavior.

3. There is tradition. Again, the evidence is mixed; however, the tendency of tradition has been to treat homosexuals with more hostility than any Christian biblical understanding would warrant. Homosexual behavior is regarded in the New Testament as but one of a vast number of symptoms of the sinfulness of humanity—no better

or worse than behaviors such as fornication, adultery, stealing, greed, drunkenness, extreme verbal abuse, and robbery.

4. There is scripture. The biblical vision of reality tells us about God, the world, and humanity in such a way that we learn how we are called to live our lives. Nevertheless, trying to determine the contemporary significance of a biblical text is not a simple matter of discerning what a passage meant in the context of its original historical situation. Scripture is a vital witness that speaks through the work of the Holy Spirit in relation to the specific dynamics of concrete historical circumstances. Thus we labor to comprehend the meaning of the Bible for our lives today. We listen to the voice of the Bible, and then under the guidance of the Spirit we ask what God requires of us as obedience.

At stake for us in our encounter with the Bible is the basic understanding of reality that anchors life, gives meaning to life, and directs our living. In Romans 1 Paul focused on God and the human situation. He wrote about God's righteousness, about God's saving grace and judging wrath; and he insisted that we humans are all powerlessly in bondage to the distorting power of sin. If we believe that Paul was right about God and humanity, then we are hard-pressed to find a persuasive argument that undermines Paul's diagnosis of homosexual activity; for Paul's statements about God, humanity, and homosexuality (as one of several indications of human sinfulness) are coherent in their style of thought and expression as they offer a theological account of the "natural" order of creation. One may deny the validity of Paul's explanation, but one cannot easily dislodge one element of the overall construction without threatening to collapse the entire exposition. Paul offers a moral assessment of social reality from a particular theological point of view; hence, his judgment of homosexuality results from his understanding of God and the human condition. We cannot fault Paul's appraisal of homosexual behavior without denying the theological vision that informs his understanding of God and humanity.

With Paul, we need to see that the point of announcing God's judgment is to declare God's prior, self-wrought reconciliation to humanity in Jesus Christ. If we have a hope, it is not the bland stuff of "I'm okay; you're okay" or "Live and let live." The gospel tells us that God loves us, despite our sinfulness. When we refuse to say a biblical word about homosexual activity in the world today, the church is in danger of taking the easy path of mere acceptance, not of struggling along the rough road of God's costly reconciliation through Jesus Christ that ultimately requires us to face and renounce our sinfulness and its evidences.

The biblical message is a clear but hopeful word to all humanity about God's will. The gospel does not come as a mere affirmation of who we are and what we do; rather, it tells us that God is the God of the ungodly, who saves us in and from our unrighteousness. God liberates us from bondage to sin for a new, complete service to righteousness; that is, we are freed from the captivating power of impure involvements as God brings us into a new relationship that frees us for obedience to God's will for our lives. By avoiding or denying the biblical word regarding homosexuality the church does not do the difficult ministry of reconciliation to which God in Jesus Christ has commissioned us. Yet, in Jesus Christ, God beckons us beyond the present patterns of our human practices, forgives our failures, and promises us wholeness in Jesus Christ in God's new creation that is coming and will come.

Jesus Christ and Sexuality

I argued in the first chapter that Jesus Christ himself must be the norm of our interpretation of scripture. But in relation to homosexuality or homosexual behavior we have no recorded word or action of Jesus himself that provides direct evidence and instruction about what we are to say and do ourselves. Remarkably, the subject of homosexuality that is so controversial for us today is a matter Jesus never addressed.

Fortunately, however, Jesus did speak about the related topic of human sexuality. He did so in the specific context of a debate about divorce, in Matt. 19:3–8 and Mark 10:2–9. Since the vast majority of scholars judges the passage in Mark to be the older form of the material, we shall focus on that text.

Mark informs the readers of the Gospel that Pharisees went to Jesus to ask him whether he thought it was lawful to divorce, and in doing so they were testing Jesus. From a careful reading of Mark's Gospel we can see what Mark means by saying that "to test him they asked. . . ." Mark 3 tells that the Pharisees and the Herodians (the political supporters of Herod Antipas) were in league so they might destroy Jesus. Then in Mark 6 John the Baptist had a confrontation with Herod Antipas over Herod's marrying Herodias, the former wife of his brother Philip, and the outcome was that Herod killed John for criticizing their behavior. At Mark 10:1 Jesus was in the Transjordan region of Perea, that is, Herod Antipas's political domain. Thus the motive of the Pharisees' testing is clear: They asked Jesus about the legality of divorce in hopes that his answer would infuriate Herod Antipas, who would then surely kill Jesus as he had killed John.

In this context of hostile controversy Jesus spoke about marriage. He showed little interest in the legal issue of divorce; instead his remarks focused on God's purposes in making humans in the form of males and females. Jesus' statements explicitly concern marriage and human sexuality rather than divorce per se. Jesus rejected the compromised position of the Pharisees (see Mark 10:3–4) and avoided a legal debate over the interpretation of Deuteronomy 24, the Mosaic passage providing for a billet of divorce to be given to a woman at the time of a legal separation from her husband. Jesus translated the conversation to a new plane. Instead of debating the validity of divorce, he declared the absolute will of God, expressed in God's purposeful creation and described in Genesis 1–2. Maleness and femaleness—that is, human sexuality—are the evidence of God's intention that males and females enter into complementary, creative sexual unions that bind them together in a divinely intended and designed new form of life.

While Jesus is not reported to have spoken on homosexuality or homosexual behavior, his one recorded statement about human sexuality reveals that he understood males and females to be created by God for mutual relations that unite and fulfill both male and female in a (permanent) complementary union. There is no room here for an argument from silence concerning what Jesus "might have" or "must have" thought about homosexuality. But from Jesus' own words we see that he understood human sexuality to be God's own creation for the purpose of male and female uniting in a complementary relationship that brought both to a new state of unity and fulfillment (in marriage). That Jesus himself was single is the clearest indication that male and female sexual union is not a necessary condition for human fulfillment. But Jesus' teaching shows that he understood heterosexual union in the context of marriage to be the norm of divinely intended human sexual behavior. Thus, judging from both Jesus' words and actions, we may conclude that marital heterosexual unions and abstinence from sexual involvement are the options for human sexual behavior that accord with the will of God. Indeed, Jesus showed even less interest in discussing homosexuality than does the Jewish culture in which he thought and lived.

Not only what Jesus said is important for Christians. I shall return subsequently to the significance of the relationship between Christians and Jesus Christ as risen Lord. Our contemporary experience of Jesus Christ as a redeeming figure forms our lives, so that what we understand about God, life, and human sexuality as a result of our relationship to the person of Jesus Christ focuses and directs our thinking and living in relation to homosexuality.

3. Thinking about the Gospel and Homosexuality

In discussions of homosexuality in the context of the Christian community, one regularly encounters the repeated assertion that "there is no *theological* reason to deny that homosexuality is a valid lifestyle for some members of the church." This declaration is heard so often as to take on the ring of self-evident truth and to call into question the opinion of those who do not agree with this position. The statement, however, is rarely if ever explained. It is made; then it is repeated again. But one must ask, What would constitute a *theological* reason for affirming or denying the validity of homosexuality as an alternative lifestyle for some Christians?

Historically, thinking is deemed to be *theological* if it has religious significance and deals with matters of faith, practice, and experience from a distinctly religious point of view. Theological thinking is reasoning that is done from a theological viewpoint. Such thinking recognizes particular authorities and carefully weighs the insights and perspectives of these authorities—scripture, tradition, experience, and reason and science—in an effort to draw conclusions that inform and direct religious belief and life. Theology itself, although a construct of the perspective of a variety of authorities, becomes a measure for judging the adequacy and authenticity of religious thoughts and actions.

When one hears that "there is no *theological* reason to deny that homosexuality is a valid lifestyle for some members of the church," one should naturally understand that the person making this statement is claiming that a balanced reflection on scripture, tradition, experience, and reason and science finds no conclusive opposition to homosexuality, or better, to the homosexual activity of some Christians. When understood in this manner, the assertion appears questionable.

As the materials in chapters 1 and 2 demonstrated, the Reformed tradition holds a high view of scripture, and, in turn, the position of scripture regarding homosexuality is univocal: The scriptures speak seldom about homosexuality, but when they do they consistently contend that homosexual activity is unacceptable behavior in the context of the communities of Israel and the church. How, then, can defenders of homosexuality state that there is no theological reason to reject homosexual behavior for some persons in the church? Their argument is based on the demonstrated need of scripture to be interpreted in order to find its relevance for the life of the church.

The Bible was not written directly to us; rather it was written to people in other times and places, so that we must interpret the meaning of the biblical statements to persons in other settings in order to grasp the meaning of scripture for us in our own situation(s). In brief, critics of the scriptural condemnation of homosexuality either dismiss the normative value of scripture or argue that the distance between the biblical world(s) and the world of today is great, and that when correctly understood, the scriptures hold no condemnation of homosexuality in the context of contemporary society and church. I shall return to this point later, for it is a crucial issue in current Christian reflection; but for now let us put that topic on hold as we take up the matters of tradition, experience, and reason and science as they inform theological consideration of homosexuality in the church today.

The Severity of Tradition

Careful analysis of the traditional attitude of the church toward homosexuality by Derrick Sherwin Bailey (*Homosexuality and the Western Christian Tradition* [London/New York/Toronto: Longmans, Green and Co., 1955], esp. 82–120), which is followed and amplified by H. Kimball Jones (*Toward a Christian Understanding of the Homosexual* [New York: Association Press, 1966], esp. 66–89), Peter Coleman (*Christian Attitudes to Homosexuality* [London: SPCK, 1980], 124–44), and others, demonstrates the "remarkably consistent" Christian attitude toward homosexual behavior "throughout church history," where "from the middle of the second century to the end of the nineteenth, the records show that homosexual offenses were declared sinful and those who were found guilty of them rigorously punished" (Coleman, *Attitudes*, 124). More recently, the revisionist history writing of John Boswell (*Christianity, Social Tolerance, and Homosexuality* [Chicago/London: University of Chicago Press, 1980]) has argued that homosexuality was tolerated, even accepted, in the Christian tradition until the mid-thirteenth century, when for a variety of reasons the church took a negative view of homosexuality and retrojected that attitude into its reading of scripture and texts of church history. Boswell's interpretation has found a following. Yet, despite much early praise from reviewers, a number of biblical scholars (see Richard B. Hays, "Relations Natural and Unnatural: A Response to John Boswell's Exegesis of Romans 1," *Journal of Religious Ethics* 14 [1986]: 184–215) and church historians (J. Robert Wright, "Boswell on Homosexuality: A Case Undemonstrated," *Anglican Theological Review* 66 [1984]: 79–94) alike have identified interpretive flaws in both his exegesis of biblical texts and his reading of historical documents that render his case untenable.

Boswell does succeed in demonstrating that the phenomenon of homosexuality has been present with Christianity through the centuries and that the church's perspectives on homosexuality have been more complex and variegated than one might assume, but his contentions that the scriptures and the first twelve hundred years of the church's history took no stance against homosexuality have not weathered the process of expert scrutiny (see Richard John Neuhaus, "The Public Square: In the Case of John Boswell," *First Things* 41 [March 1994]: 56–59; and further, Robin Darling Young, "Gay Marriage: Reimagining Church History," *First Things* 47 [November 1994]: 43–48). Even scholars who praise Boswell's "courage and candor" have sharply faulted him for misquoting, misinterpreting, and citing texts out of their sensible contexts (Michael M. Sheehan, "Christianity and Homosexuality," *Journal of Ecclesiastical History* 33 [1982]: 438–46, esp. 441–46). Mere reference to Boswell's work can no longer pass as verification of the claim that there was no serious opposition to homosexuality in scripture and in the initial centuries of the church's history. A more accurate summary of the positions of scripture and church history toward homosexuality is Peter Coleman's observation "that the problem of homosexual behavior was never absent and required periodic denunciation" (*Attitudes*, 124).

The New Testament Era

As we saw above, in the earliest period of Christian writing Paul expressed the traditional Jewish rejection of homosexual behavior in the new context of the Christian community. There is no evidence that his remarks were made in situations where there would have been disagreement with his point of view. Many of Paul's religious contentions were controversial, deemed by some other first-century Christians to be dangerously liberal (for example, his advocating Gentile Christian freedom from law observance, his emphasis on grace that suggested to some a lack of concern with sin, and his charismatic style of ministry that led him to alter plans so that he seemed fickle). It is remarkable that the same Paul who was judged by conservative Christians of his own time to be an iconoclast is today perceived to be unimaginatively, artificially, or oppressively conservative with regard to the matter of homosexuality. We should note, however, in the context of first-century Christianity that the liberal Paul's obviously negative assessment of homosexual behavior was not the source of controversy and met with no opposition. We should recognize that Paul's references to homosexual behavior were mere illustrations of the sinful behavior of an idolatrous humanity, but we should see that Paul's remarks about homosexual behavior were made in such a way that he simply assumed other early Christians would have agreed with him that homosexual acts were not permissible among the members of the church. Paul made no attempt to defend or to respond to criticism of his position on homosexuality. Thus, from the limited instances in which earliest Christian literature treats homosexuality, we see plainly that homosexual behavior was rejected, that it was considered contrary to the will of God for human life.

The Early Church Period

The evidence from the time following the decades in which the New Testament was composed yields an equally negative assessment of homosexuality. Early Christian authors were generally concerned for "stable monogamous marriage among the Christians, and the avoidance of fornication, adultery, and all forms of unchastity" (Coleman, *Attitudes*, 126–27). A range of authors including Justin Martyr, Tertullian, Basil of Caesarea, Gregory of Nyssa, the participants in the Councils of Elvira and Ancyra, the author(s) of the *Apostolic Constitutions*, John Chrysostom, and Augustine all expressed sharp disapproval of homosexual behavior. At times these authors echoed the images and reasoning of the Old Testament condemnations of homosexuality and reiterated Paul's teaching on the subject. Yet at other times the rhetoric against homosexuality was amplified and the biblical condemnation was intensified as Sodom became a symbol for homosexuality per se, which was denounced as "wickedness . . . contrary to nature" (*Apostolic Constitutions* 7.2). Augustine's harsh comments about homosexual behavior as lustful activity that ostracizes humans from God (see his *Confessions* 3.8.15) are seemingly bridled in comparison with Chrysostom's castigation of homosexuality as depravity that results from a life of licentious luxury (summarized in Coleman, *Attitudes*, 128–29 with reference to Chrysostom's fourth *Homily on Romans*). Even Basil and Gregory were stern in their judgment of homosexual behavior, declaring that it was comparable to adultery and more serious than the otherwise grave sin of fornication (see esp. Basil's *Epistle* 217 canon 62).

Summarizing the situation in early Christianity, David F. Wright concludes,

The church fathers universally condemned male homosexual behavior. In a standard triad of sexual sins that
includes adultery and fornication, *arsenokoitia* (same
root as Paul's term) appears interchangeably with
paidophthoria ("perversion of boys". . .). Although the
Levitical prohibition was not frequently cited . . . , no
evidence suggests that it was felt to be no longer bind-
ing or to condemn only ceremonial uncleanness. Many
fathers emphasized the homosexual lusts of the
Sodomites. . . . Some criticized other aspects of their depravity, but no patristic source excludes a homosexual
interpretation of their conduct. . . .

All the evidence indicates that the teaching mind of
the early church unreservedly condemned homosexual
activity. Yet, although clearly viewed as contrary to
God's will in scripture and nature, it was not singled out
for special execration ("Homosexuality," in E. Ferguson
et al., eds., *Encyclopedia of Early Christianity* [New York/
London: Garland, 1990], 435–36).

The Medieval Church

The early church's severe criticism of homosexuality
was inherited by and grew harsher in the church during
the Middle Ages. During the period of early Christianity,
at two prominent councils of the early church, Elvira in
Spain (305–306 C.E.) and Ancyra in Asia Minor (314 C.E.),
homosexuals had been denied baptism and catechetical
status until they renounced their behavior; and Basil of
Caesarea (375 C.E.) was typical of the early period when he
called for fifteen years of penance before those engaging in
homosexual acts would be permitted to receive the sacra-
ments—a penalty similar in severity to that given to adulterers, whereas fornicators were required to do seven years
of penance.

Attitudes toward homosexual behavior frequently
grew more severe in later periods, however, so that in

Spain about 650 C.E. regulations held that homosexuals were to be castrated. This stipulation was reiterated about forty years later by the king of Gothic Spain, Egica, at the sixteenth Council of Toledo in 693 C.E. While it is not possible to reconstruct a simple linear development in the assessment of homosexual acts, it is helpful to trace the evidence through time, for later writers often demonstrate specific, even thorough, knowledge of pronouncements from periods prior to their own. By following the declarations of authorities through time we can see something of the complexity of the attitudes toward homosexuality in the tradition(s) of the medieval church.

The most complete treatment of various homosexual acts and the punishments that were deemed appropriate for them are found in the collection of writings usually designated as the *Penitentials* (see J. T. McNeill and H. M. Gamer, eds., *Medieval Handbooks of Penance,* Records of Civilization 29 [New York: Columbia University Press, 1938]). These works were of Celtic origin, but they spread and developed through Western Christendom from about 570 to 1010 C.E. The most famous of these regulations are ascribed to Theodore of Tarsus, the archbishop of Canterbury, about 670 C.E. The *Penitentials* compile a list of sins that is intended to be exhaustive and, in turn, prescribe the appropriate punishment or penance. A noticeable portion of the *Penitentials* delineates the range of homosexual behaviors and defines penance deemed appropriate to the acts. Punishments vary from observing eight special fasts for simple homosexual kissing to twenty to forty days of penance for mutual masturbation by first-time offenders to two years' penance for interfemoral connection to seven years penance for habitual fellatio and for sodomy. The *Penitentials* were remarkable for their differentiation of homosexual acts and for recognizing and condemning lesbianism (although the latter phenomenon was not treated with the thoroughness given to male homosexuality).

Independent of the *Penitentials,* an ordinance of Aix-la-Chapelle (Aachen) from 789 C.E. cited the position of the Council of Ancyra to articulate a general condemnation of homosexuality. Similar denunciations occurred during the 800s, one coming from Charlemagne himself that dealt with sodomy among monks. Yet these declarations were vague in defining and decrying homosexual activity.

Sharp criticism came in 1051 C.E. from Peter Damian, abbot of Fonte-Avellino, who published *Liber Gomorrhianus* in condemnation of various homosexual acts. He described these activities as ranging in severity from mutual masturbation to interfemoral connection to sodomy. Damian called for penalties in keeping with the gravity of the deeds, but his every denunciation was harsh. He criticized the regulations of the *Penitentials,* which he found lax, and called for maximum penalties for all homosexual acts, since they were all sins against nature. Damian referred to Basil's observations about homosexual activity with tempered approval and then insisted that any monk or clergy engaging in such acts must be removed from their orders. His invectives were so acrimonious that an outcry of protests ultimately caused Pope Leo IX to restrain Damian's severity, although Leo had originally received *Liber Gomorrhianus* with approval. Leo's technique was to praise Damian's motivation in advocating chastity and denouncing vice but to condemn his harsh attitude toward those committing the unacceptable acts. Thus Leo gave no quarter to homosexual activity, although he did not impose the harsh sanctions for which Damian had called.

During the twelfth century there were a variety of judgments concerning homosexual activities. At the Council of London at Westminster in 1102 C.E. those engaging in "the shameful sin of sodomy" were condemned by anathema until they demonstrated through confession and penance that they were worthy of absolution. Through the weekly publication of their condemnation, those who were so punished by excommunication were exposed publicly "in all churches throughout the land," that is, in the whole realm of England (canon 28 of the Council of London; cited in Bailey, *Homosexuality*, 124). In 1120 C.E., however, at a council held at Neapolis (today's Nablus, Jordan; near ancient Shechem in Palestine), both the king and the patriarch of Jerusalem issued stern condemnation of homosexuality, calling for persons defiling themselves voluntarily through sodomy—active or passive—to be burned at the stake. Here the church yielded the enactment of the punishment of sodomists to the civil authorities, granting tacit approval to such executions although not implementing such punishment directly. Furthermore, at the third Lateran Council in 1179 C.E. a canon (session 3.11) denounced "incontinence contrary to nature"—meaning homosexual behaviors—and that ruling was reiterated subsequently in church writings for the next century.

The thirteenth century saw further developments. First, like many before him, Thomas Aquinas differentiated degrees of sexual impropriety. His treatment of the subject was not detailed, but he ranked only bestiality as being more grievous than sodomy. He judged homosexual acts to be direct violations of the divine law by which all human life is to be controlled. He reasoned that since the natural purpose of the sexual organs is procreation, all homosexual activity is unnatural, lustful, and sinful. Although he held that the various homosexual acts might differ in the degree of their sinful gravity, he considered the least sinful homosexual act more sinful than any other kind of lust. Homosexual acts were contraventions of the order of nature that actually did injury to the Creator. Thus according to Thomas—and much of subsequent moral theology—differentiation of the species of homosexual acts serves no purpose for the work of confession. All such acts are gravely sinful; hence Thomas's logic dismantled the disciplinary system of the *Penitentials* with graded penance for graduated levels of sin.

Second, the degree of influence of the earlier ecclesiastical denunciations of homosexual acts (at least in England) is seen in the position taken in a treatise on English common law from the late 1200s, *Fleta and Britton,* wherein sodomy was simply marked as a capital crime.

The Reformation

As Peter Coleman observes, despite the "freedom" brought by the Reformation from the oppressive and legalistic casuistry of the church of the late Middle Ages, "in sexual ethics the re-enhanced primacy of the Scriptures ensured that there was no great change" (*Attitudes,* 133). Monks married, but the condemnation of homosexual activity continued.

Remarkably, if his writings are an indication of his concerns, Martin Luther seemed little interested in homosexuality. At points Luther followed the biblical interpretations of Nicholas of Lyssa, who as a Jewish convert to Christianity had written around 1300 and often preserved traditional Jewish attitudes and interpretations of biblical passages. In his lectures on Romans, Luther commented in part on Romans 1 by saying, "The body is disgraced and degraded most viciously not only by adultery and similar violations of chastity, but all the more by the degrading perversions [of those who are effeminate and who are abusers of themselves with mankind]."

John Calvin commented on Genesis by denouncing the atrocious crime of the men of Sodom who demanded "to know" the men who visited Lot and so brought on the justifiable destruction of the city. In turn, he commented on Rom. 1:27 that "even the brute beasts abhor" homosexual acts; and on 1 Cor. 6:9 he wrote,

> By *effeminate* persons I understand those who, although they do not openly abandon themselves to impurity, discover, nevertheless, their unchastity by blandishments of speech, by lightness of gesture and apparel, and other allurements. The [other] description of crime is the most abominable of all—that monstrous pollution which was but all too prevalent in Greece [abusers of themselves with mankind].

After the Reformation

As Coleman observed, sexual ethics underwent no great change as a result of the Reformation. Not only did the Protestant church with its emphasis on scriptural authority maintain the traditional position regarding homosexual acts, but also the evidence shows that the Roman Catholic Church's position did not change during or after the Reformation. One sees the continuity of the Roman Catholic stance in a pronouncement found in a document approved in 1975 by Pope Paul VI as an authoritative statement of the church. The decree is titled "Declaration on Certain Questions concerning Sexual Ethics," and it denounces homosexual behavior by referring to Romans, 1 Corinthians, and 1 Timothy to state that homosexual acts are by nature morally reprehensible and cannot be approved in any way.

During the twentieth century there has been a shift of position—primarily on the part of Protestants—regarding homosexuality. At times the new thinking has been official or at least quasi-official. While Karl Barth could describe homosexuality as "physical, psychological and social sickness, the phenomenon of perversion, decadence and decay, which can emerge when man refuses to admit the validity of the divine command" (*Church Dogmatics*, III/4, 166), Helmut Thielicke argued that "an ethical value judgment can distort even the phenomenality of the thing which is to be evaluated" (*The Ethics of Sex* [New York: Harper & Row, 1964], 271); thus he cited D. S. Bailey with approval in order to suggest that

> with a careful analysis of the medical facts and a thoughtful evaluation of the biblical and traditional statements . . . , [Bailey] arrives at the thesis that in those cases in which the personality structure cannot be altered by medical treatment the most effective help is that "which enables the person to accept his handicap as a task that must be endured in a positive spirit" (*Ethics*, 273; citing Bailey, "Homosexualität," *Religion in Geschichte und Gegenwart*, 3: 441ff.).

Thus, in the face of Christian tradition—as recited by Barth—without offering a simple endorsement or affirmation of homosexual acts, Thielicke makes a strong case for social and religious toleration of homosexuality; hence understanding rather than denunciation was to be the Christian norm with regard to homosexuality.

Others have gone farther toward affirming homosexuality. A committee of the Society of Friends in England argued in 1963 "that homosexuality in itself is a quite natural, morally neutral condition which can be used for either good or evil, and which should be no more deplored than left-handedness" (Jones, *Understanding*, 75). In like manner, the Rev. Robert Wood of the United Church of Christ in America sharply criticizes the church's attitude toward sex that, in his opinion, sullied it in order to control it. Instead of a negative assessment of homosexuality, Wood asserts that homosexuality is a glorious gift from God that provides a natural solution to the earth's population crisis. He states that homosexuals should be welcomed into the church and its ministry without any requirement that they change their pattern of sexual behavior; he suggests that the church should sponsor definite activities designed to serve homosexuals, for example, promoting "drag" dances; and the church should conduct marriage ceremonies for homosexual partners who determine to relate to each other in love and devotion (see R. W. Wood, *Christ and the Homosexual* [New York: Vantage, 1960]).

Nevertheless, others continue in a serious and scholarly vein to maintain a position closer to the historical lines of Christian tradition. On the Protestant side one finds, for example, the writings of Richard B. Hays ("Relations Natural and Unnatural: A Response to John Boswell's Exegesis of Romans 1," *Journal of Religious Ethics* 14 [1986]: 184–215; "Awaiting the Redemption of Our Bodies," *Sojourners* 20 [July 1991]: 17–21). Hays holds a high view of scripture while clearly calling for the compassionate treatment of homosexuals by other Christians. The current Roman Catholic position finds expression in a defense against the accusation that "contraception, direct sterilization, autoeroticism, pre-marital sexual relations, homosexual relations and artificial inseminations were condemned as morally unacceptable" because the traditional conception of the natural law presents "as moral laws what are in themselves mere biological laws" (John Paul II, Encyclical Letter, "The Splendor of Truth," no. 47). In response to this criticism, John Paul II replies that contemporary moral theory about humanity and freedom "contradicts the

Church's teachings on the unity of the person" ("Splendor," no. 48), and

> is contrary to the teaching of Scripture and Tradition, [according to which] Saint Paul declares that "the immoral, idolaters, adulterers, sexual perverts, thieves, the greedy, drunkards, revilers, robbers" are excluded from the Kingdom of God (cf. 1 Cor 6:9). This condemnation—repeated by the Council of Trent—lists as "mortal sins" or "immoral practices" certain specific kinds of behaviour the willful acceptance of which prevents believers from sharing the inheritance promised to them ("Splendor," no. 49).

Summary of the
Findings about Tradition

This brief survey recognizes the long-standing Christian disavowal of homosexual activities. Across the centuries, the traditional Christian position toward homosexual behavior varied in severity, but was consistently negative. Only recently does one observe a shift in attitudes, although a simple poll of opinions among Christians finds that the traditional reservation about homosexual activities also characterizes the current Christian opinion about homosexuality. But there is still nothing approaching unanimity of opinion in the Christian community on this subject. The recent tendency to admit an ethically ambiguous status to homosexuality has not mitigated the traditionally negative, even harsh, assessment of such behavior by the majority of the members of the Christian community.

Nonetheless, serious reflection upon scripture will *not* support the intensely negative understanding and treatment of persons participating in homosexual acts that is prominent in Christian tradition. The approach of

Thielicke that was described above is much closer to the spirit of scripture than is the harsh assessment of much of tradition. Scripture judges homosexual behavior sinful, one kind of evidence of the sinful condition of all humanity, albeit a particularly graphic example of the idolatrous tendency of all persons to put self or some element of creation above God. Paul, who voices the most explicit disapproval of homosexual acts in the New Testament, does not single out homosexual behavior for special condemnation; rather, he regards it as a simple example of the broken, sinful condition of a segment of all of broken, sinful humanity.

The Ambiguity of Experience

Experience is perhaps the most problematic of the "authorities" for theological reflection, since as a dynamic element informing thought it is simultaneously objective and subjective. To put the problem another way, all experiences are not equal. Which experiences count? Why? Why not? Do all persons perceive the same moments and events exactly the same way? Whose perceptions are most valid?

Ancient versus Modern Homosexuality

A powerful argument in the logic of those advocating the unconditional acceptance of homosexual persons into the Christian community despite the biblical injunctions against homosexual activities is that the form of homosexuality that the biblical authors knew about, experienced, and commented upon is unlike forms of homosexuality that persons in the world today know and experience. The Bible is said to reflect its cultural settings, assumptions, and attitudes. In this line, Robin Scroggs focuses on the use of the Bible—particularly the New Testament—in the contemporary consideration of homosexuality. Scroggs presents a model of homosexual culture in the Greco-Roman world that he argues was the only one Paul and the early church would have known, namely, the practice of pederasty.

Scroggs does not mean to suggest that pederasty was the only form of homosexuality in antiquity, rather that pederasty was the only *model* of homosexual activity available in the culture in which the early church existed. Thus he contends that the New Testament is denouncing pederasty, which was essentially oppressive, exploitative, shameful, and dehumanizing. Scroggs avers that the New Testament has nothing to say concerning other models of homosexuality that are known to twentieth-century persons but that were unknown to citizens of the first-century Mediterranean world. As he puts the issue:

> The *fact* remains, however, that the basic model in today's Christian homosexual community is so different from the model attacked by the New Testament that the criterion of reasonable similarity of context is not met. The conclusion I have to draw seems inevitable: *Biblical judgments against homosexuality are not relevant to today's debate.* They should no longer be used in denominational discussions about homosexuality, should in no way be a weapon to justify refusal of ordination, *not because the Bible is not authoritative,* but simply because it does not address the issues involved (*New Testament and Homosexuality,* [Philadelphia: Fortress, 1983], 127).

The evidence, however, is not what Scroggs would have it to be. He protests that he does "not wish to use Procrustes' bed to force all male homosexual activities in the Greco-Roman world to a simple form of pederasty [for he does] not doubt that friendships of good passion and tender caring existed" (*New Testament and Homosexuality*, 139). Yet Scroggs's contention that pederasty was the only model of homosexuality known in antiquity is simplistic and misleading. Peter Coleman surveyed "Greek and Roman attitudes to homosexuality," and after a careful weighing of the evidence available from prominent Greek sources (mythologies, Plato, and Aristotle), he concluded,

> Homosexuality among the Greeks is well attested by the fifth-century philosophers as a normal and valuable relationship, chiefly associated with private tuition, and the concepts of friendship. Commercial exploitation and pederasty especially among older men and immature boys was disapproved (*Attitudes*, 120).

Long before the period of the New Testament the Greeks showed themselves capable of distinguishing pederasty from other homosexual behaviors or "models," and they condemned it as an unacceptable model of sexual behavior while offering forms of praise for other kinds of homosexual relationships.

More relevant to the time of the New Testament is the Roman period, and there the matter is even clearer in the Latin sources. Both satirists and historians held a high view of family that was typical of Roman culture in general. Nevertheless, from such writings one finds that adultery and sodomy occurred among the affluent and leisurely classes of citizens, including the ruling class. Licentiousness, especially homosexual acts, met with popular disapproval. According to Suetonius, Julius Caesar was at the beginning of his adult life the catamite to the king of Bithynia (a country in ancient Asia Minor):

> He [Julius] served his first campaign in Asia on the personal staff of Marcus Thermus, governor of the

province. Being sent by Thermus to Bithynia . . . he daw-
dled so long at the court of Nicodemes that he was sus-
pected of improper relations with the king; and he lent
colour to this scandal by going back to Bithynia a few
days after his return, with the alleged purpose of col-
lecting a debt for a freedman, one of his dependents.
During the rest of his campaign he enjoyed a better reputation (*Lives of the Caesars* 1.2).

This segment of his career became, however, a political li-
ability and the subject of vulgar behavior among Julius's
own troops. Regarding developments during the year 45
B.C.E., Suetonius writes,

There was no stain on his reputation for chastity except
his intimacy with King Nicodemes, but that was a deep
and lasting reproach, which laid him open to insults
from every quarter. I say nothing of the notorious lines
of Licinius Calvus: "Whate'er Bithynia had, and Caesar's paramour." I pass over, too, the invectives of Dolabella and the elder Curio, in which Dolabella calls him
"the queen's rival, the inner partner of the royal couch,"
and Curio, "the brothel of Nicodemes and the stew of
Bithynia." . . . of the edicts of Bibulus, in which he
posted his colleague as "the queen of Bithynia," saying
that "of yore he was enamoured of a king, but now of a
king's estate." . . . Octavius, a man whose disordered
mind made him somewhat free with his tongue, after
saluting Pompey as "king" in a crowded assembly,
greeted Caesar as "queen." . . . Cicero . . . [wrote] that
Caesar was led by the king's attendants to the royal
apartments, that he lay on a golden couch arrayed in
purple, and that the virginity of this son of Venus was
lost in Bithynia: . . . Finally, in his Gallic triumph his sol-
diers, among the bantering songs which are usually
sung by those who follow the chariot, shouted these
lines, which became a by-word: "All the Gauls did Caesar vanquish, Nicodemes vanquished him; Lo! now
Caesar rides in triumph, victor over the Gauls,

Nicodemes does not triumph, who subdued the con-
queror" (*Lives* 1.49).

I have quoted these reports at length to show that Romans
knew and had clear disdain for forms of homosexuality
other than pederasty. Julius Caesar and King Nicodemes
were, in modern parlance, two consenting adults, and
their behavior was scandalous and roundly ridiculed.

Scroggs's case collapses upon scrutiny of the historical
evidence. Moreover, despite Scroggs's contentions, nothing in the New Testament writings suggests that pederasty
per se was being singled out from among other forms of
homosexual activity for special condemnation. The New
Testament authors simply viewed all homosexual acts as
being cut of one cloth, and they denounced all garments
made of that material.

Thinking across the Ages

A slightly more subtle argument is offered by Victor
Paul Furnish in a chapter on "Homosexuality" in *The
Moral Teaching of Paul* (Nashville: Abingdon, 1979). One
might consider Furnish's study under the rubric of "reason" rather than "experience," but since he works with the
idea of the distance between ancient and modern experiences of homosexuality that focused Scroggs's work, I
shall examine his contribution at this point.

After a judicious analysis of the pertinent passages in
the Pauline epistles, Furnish summarizes:

The pattern of thought in Romans 1:18–32 should now
be clear. It is a denunciation of the Gentiles formulated
in accord with Jewish reasoning. . . . This is their sin,
their attempt to exist apart from God. In consequence,
God has now been "revealed" to them through his

wrath (see Rom. 1:18), and the vices typical of Gentile
society are the specific evidences of this. . . . Homosexual intercourse is mentioned as one of these typically
Gentile practices (1:26b-27) *(Teaching,* 77–78).

Reflecting on Paul's teaching about homosexuality, Furnish makes several observations:

Paul condemns homosexual practices. However, he is
not preoccupied with this matter . . . and there is no evidence that he ever had to deal with a specific case of
homosexual conduct. . . . Since Paul offered no direct
teaching to his own churches on the subject of homosexual conduct, his letters certainly cannot yield any
specific answers to the questions being faced in the
modern church. . . .
    But what Paul accepted as a matter of course about
homosexual behavior, we can no longer take for
granted. . . . one must now acknowledge that homosexuality is an exceedingly complex phenomenon. . . . homosexuality has multiple causes . . . psychological . . . social
factors . . . perhaps even some biological conditions . . .
the forms and evidences of homosexuality are now understood to be many and varied. . . .
    It would be unfair to charge Paul with naïveté or ig-
norance in the matter of homosexuality. Such evidence
as we have suggests he was as informed as anyone
could have been in his day. Indeed, *we* should be the
naïve ones were we to ignore the data available to us in
our own day, supposing that Paul's teaching alone is
sufficient to answer our questions about right and
wrong in this difficult matter *(Teaching,* 79–81).

While Furnish offers further elaborations to his conclusions, it is clear that he finds Paul's experience of homosexuality and the twentieth-century experience of the
phenomenon sufficiently different to render Paul's comments less than fully authoritative and relevant. Yet one
could make the same argument about almost any topic on

which Paul ever wrote. Paul's observations about drunkenness, greed, dishonesty, adultery, sin, forgiveness, reconciliation, and even God are all time bound and uninformed of the latest psychological, sociological, and biological data; but remarkably few persons are willing to conclude that Paul's lack of certain information on these issues puts him in an inferior position with regard to authoritative theological knowledge about such matters. That Paul derived his teachings from revelation is, of course, debated; but faith in revelation as a source of Paul's teachings does not have to remain uninformed of the insights of human experience any more than a concern with empirical data has to ignore the claims of faith.

Nevertheless, the temptation simply to explain Paul's teachings away by relativizing them to the past is always at hand. When we find Paul or other scriptures speaking in a variety of voices (for example, on matters of clean and unclean foods, marriage, divorce, women's leadership in the church, head coverings, personal adornment, etc.), we are bound to seek an authoritative word in the chorus of witnesses; but if we take biblical authority with utter seriousness, we are never at liberty to dismiss scripture altogether, much less to set aside a univocal biblical declaration of God's will and purposes. The Bible may speak seldom about homosexual behavior—as it does about murder and incest—but when we hear scripture's one voice on this (and other subjects) we cannot simply attribute what we hear to an uninformed or outdated point of view and then set it aside in favor of a position more compatible with the perspectives of the time in which we live. It is entirely possible that the Bible has nothing to say about a particular subject, but when the scriptures do speak to a topic, particularly with one voice, we in the Reformed tradition are bound to struggle with the texts to discern with as much clarity as possible what the Bible means for us today.

Furnish himself never simply dismisses scripture, but he comes perilously close when he writes:

> It is no longer possible to share Paul's belief that homosexual conduct always and necessarily involves [a rebellion against the Creator and his creation, a surrender to one's own lusts, the debasement of one's own true identity and the exploitation of another's]" (*Teaching*, 81).

Of course, as he recognizes, Furnish does not know what he says here from the Bible; moreover, Paul does not contradict himself at other points in his writings, nor do other portions of scripture offer an assessment of homosexual activities that differs from Paul's. Rather, Furnish's comments show that he developed the position he expresses here by consulting the modern experience of homosexuality as viewed from the perspectives of psychology, sociology, and perhaps biology—an experience that he apparently judges to offer better information than the texts of scripture on this issue and at this point in time. Elizabeth R. Achtemeier comments on such logic bluntly:

> Only if one turns to other authorities besides the Scriptures can one approve of the practice [of homosexuality], but then, of course, the church's one authority for faith and practice, namely the Bible, has been abandoned, and we are adrift on every sea of fancy and folly ("Homosexuality: What Does the Bible Say?" *reSOURCE* [May 1993]: 15).

Furthermore, Furnish attempts to strike a balanced view of sinfulness in sexual behavior when he observes that "it can be said with certainty that whenever a homosexual *or* heterosexual relationship does involve one or more of these [lust, debasement, exploitation], it stands under the judgment of scripture" (*Teaching*, 81). He is correct; but Furnish fails to recognize that heterosexual abuses do not guarantee the validity of more decorous homosexual behaviors.

Experience as Verification

Still others argue differently from experience to establish that homosexual activity is not necessarily unacceptable in the context of Christian community. They point to the clear and undeniable manifestations of grace in the lives of homosexual persons in the church. Homosexual ministers are held up as models of compassionate Christian living. Gifts for preaching, teaching, caring, and leading are cited among homosexual Christians. Long-term committed partnerships are mentioned as illustrations of permanent, monogamous, loving relationships—a noteworthy phenomenon in an age when heterosexual divorce is a commonplace. Contrasts are made between effective homosexuals who live and minister with integrity and decadent heterosexuals who live solipsistically and feign ministry through manipulation. But for every story about noble Christian life on the part of a homosexual, one can find a sordid tale of homosexual depravity—in the same way that both truly godly and terribly ungodly behavior can characterize the lives of various heterosexuals.

That God manifests grace in conditions of human brokenness is the message of the Christian gospel. But grace observed in brokenness is no endorsement or vindication of the human condition; rather, it is sheer evidence of the magnificence of God's grace that finds strength in weakness as God labors to reconcile a broken and sinful humanity through the gospel of Jesus Christ. Experience must inform theological reflection, but a theology of experience is dangerously subjective.

Scripture itself is a kind of Spirit-inspired witness to the grace-filled experience of persons whose lives were dramatically influenced by God. Life's experiences in our world today—for the purposes of the current debate over homosexuality in the context of the church, a world no more than forty years old—cannot automatically be given precedence over the message of the Bible. Our cultural perspective is not inherently superior to the worldview(s) and attitude(s) of biblical culture(s). A theologically valid assessment of homosexual behavior can as easily have been given in first-century (and earlier) terms as in those of the twentieth century. For people affirming biblical authority, the past may be given theological, if not historical and cultural, priority over the present. Yet the experience of the past should not simply control the present—that would be an operation contrary to the truth of the gospel—but the present is not necessarily the lord over the past. God stands in and over both past and present, and God adjudicates the relationship between humanity's experiences of God now and then.

The Reasonable Desire
of Christian Compassion

When confronted with the complex phenomenon of homosexuality as it is known in the twentieth century, Christians (and, of course, many others) find themselves in a quandary. Peter Coleman has described the difficulty as "a clash of loyalties":

> Unlike many other claims to basic human rights, to which Christian conscience has freely responded in

recent years, the request from homosexual people that they should be left free to express their sexual difference in the particular ways open to them seems disconcerting.

It is not proving at all easy for heterosexual Christians to agree to this change . . . [and] the limits of tolerance have shifted back and forth in recent years. Those limits are not set by fashion, nor by moral codes and laws, but by loyalties. There is a proper loyalty Christians give to the teaching of the Bible and the tradition of the church. There is also a proper loyalty Christians give to any brother or sister in need, without such loyalty faith is dead. When a gay Christian asks for acceptance, those loyalties appear to clash (*Gay Christians: A Moral Dilemma* [London: SCM; Philadelphia: Trinity Press International, 1989], xii).

Many Christians easily recognize that simply being heterosexual in not a necessary good. The world knows heterosexual relationships that are abusive, oppressive, inequitable, and unjust from the vantage point of God's purposes as we know them from God's involvement with humanity down through history as recorded in scripture. Moreover, many heterosexual Christians recognize that homosexuality is not a simple monolithic phenomenon. People may desire or engage in homosexual relations for many of the same reasons that other persons want or take part in heterosexual relations. Thus many Christians with strong loyalties to the Bible and to the traditions of the church have reasonable reservations about the quick and easy condemnation of homosexuality. They experience a clash of sensibilities that is disconcerting, and the temptation to find an easy way out of this deep discomfort is real: Homosexuality is often quickly rejected, quickly affirmed, or more often, quickly tolerated with little further reflection.

Reasonable Reservations

Both logic and the findings of contemporary sciences may give rise to reasonable reservations about the biblical and traditional disapproval of homosexuality. First, the protests of straightforward logic include:

1. "The Bible is not a rule book." This observation is correct, and a simple use of the scriptures as if they were mere moral and social prescriptions and prohibitions fails to recognize the complexity of the biblical canon. Nonetheless, the scriptures do present and advocate a worldview that is held to be authoritative and trustworthy for the formation and living of Christian life. The Levitical codes come close to making rules for life, although Old Testament experts view the regulations of Leviticus as standards of holiness, directives for the formation of community life, aimed at establishing and maintaining a people's identity in relation to God. The materials of Leviticus have even been compared to a form of ancient pastoral care, so that people are privileged to "imitate the divine" (John H. Hayes, "Leviticus," *Harper's Bible Commentary* [San Francisco: Harper & Row, 1988], 175). Moreover, Paul's teachings as preserved through the epistles of the New Testament are never mere rules; rather, Paul presented a vision of God, the world, and human existence that he challenged his audiences to embrace and to live. Both Leviticus and Paul understand, however, that accepting, affirming, and living out a particular theological worldview means that there are acceptable and unacceptable behaviors for those concerned to live in a positive relation to God. The Bible is not a rule book, but it presents a way of looking at life that holds some patterns of life to be unacceptable and other patterns of life to be sanctioned by God.

2. "There are few references to homosexual behavior in the Bible." Here the reasoning seems to be that the relatively infrequent treatment of the phenomenon of homosexuality in scripture makes it a marginal issue that can be tolerated. But this reasoning is fragile. There is also little about rape in the Bible; Paul never mentions the topic. But no one should attempt to argue for the acceptability of this purely deplorable and ungodly phenomenon because of the meager number of times the Bible addresses the matter. The general theological worldview of scripture supports strong denunciation of rape, incest, murder, drunkenness, bestiality, and a host of other items that the Bible mentions only a few times.

3. "Toleration seems preferable to an unwillingness to grant equal rights to homosexuals" and "acceptance seems more loving than rejection." Both these observations are true, but neither toleration of homosexuals that would grant them equal civil rights nor acceptance that reaches out and deals with homosexuals with compassion, concern, care, and love requires condonation or approval of homosexual activity. Christian disapproval of homosexuality does not—cannot and should not—mean social intolerance and religious rejection of homosexuals as citizens with equal rights and children of God. As Richard Hays has written,

> If homosexual persons are not welcome in the church, I will have to walk out the door along with them, leaving in the sanctuary only those entitled to cast the first stone.
> We live, then, as a community that embraces sinners as Jesus did, without waiving God's righteousness. We live confessing that God's grace claims us out of confusion and alienation and sets about making us whole. We live knowing that wholeness remains a hope rather than

an attainment in this life ("Awaiting the Redemption of Our Bodies," *Sojourners* 20 [July 1991]: 21).

Second, the data of psychology, sociology, physiology, and biology concerning homosexuality raise difficult questions about the origins, causes, and motivations of homosexual behavior. Many Christian thinkers contend the evidences of science have brought us into a new situation regarding the understanding of homosexuality. They reason that our superior current information gives us an advantage over the authors of scripture, so that we may move with newfound confidence away from the biblical and traditional disapproval of homosexuality.

Yet the information on homosexuality offered by the sciences is ambiguous, always open to interpretation, often contradictory, and sometimes misleading. Anyone who has read newspaper articles on homosexuality has encountered the confused state of information on the subject. Moreover, the descriptive information provided by the sciences, at best, tells us how things *are*, not how things *ought to be*. Scripture never attempts to locate the origin of homosexual behavior other than in the power of sin; that is, such behavior results from the operation of the force of evil at work in the world in opposition to God. This contention may seem severe, but it is a theological position that is not simply vulnerable to the critique of science. The natural, physical, and human sciences have no instruments to analyze the power of sin—especially if sin is not reduced to the sum total of human misdeeds plus the catastrophes found in nature. Paul presents sin as a terrible force that has enslaved humanity "in the flesh" in the parameters of broken creation and that distorts all creation from the life for which God created it. Moreover, Paul says God is at work through the gracious mystery of Jesus Christ saving humanity from the dreadful condition in which all humans are bound. The sciences may offer nontheological theories of existence and set them over against Paul's presentation, but they cannot critique Paul's theological picture.

Attempts at Resolution through Hermeneutics

Christians often attempt to eliminate the problem of homosexuality by finding ways to approve of homosexual behavior. Some view homosexuality under the rubrics of prominent biblical themes to argue for approval of homosexual activity. *Love* is named as the motive and power for sanctioning homosexual behavior in the lives of members of the church. Love becomes, however, merely approving acceptance. This is a false definition of love. When Jesus came face to face with the scribes and the Pharisees and the woman who had been caught in adultery, he loved her. He confronted her self-righteous accusers, and he accepted and forgave her, saying, "Go, and do not sin again." Jesus did not say, "I do not condemn you; go, and do what you were doing—go, and do as you please." Love offered and demanded change.

Similarly, a desire for *justice* calls for the endorsement of homosexual behavior; here justice is equated with fairness or equitable treatment. I have already argued that the biblical condemnation of homosexuality does not mean social or civil intolerance of homosexual individuals; indeed, the gospel directs Christians to relate in compassion and concern to all persons, for we are all sinners. A strong Christian argument for fairness suggests nothing about condoning homosexual behavior. Justice as a biblical concept, however, is far more than fairness. Indeed, biblical justice means bringing the structures of reality into compliance with God's will. The same Bible that repeats God's call for justice also repeats a theological disapproval of homosexual behavior. We destroy the power of biblical logic when we bifurcate biblical language to have a call for justice amount to a call to approve of homosexuality as an act of fairness. (The same reply can be made to the recent calls for "doing justice-love," yet another hermeneutic using biblical language against the plain sense of the texts of the Bible.)

Liberation is another biblical category presented as the reason that the church should approve of homosexuality. But again we may recall Jesus' words to the woman caught in adultery, "Go, and do not sin again." Humans are liberated from sin for freedom to relate to God in a new way. We learn of the good of liberation from the Bible, which teaches that homosexual behavior is the result of the power of sin over human life. The biblical call for liberation and Jesus' own granting of freedom are related to sin. If the biblical definition of sin and the biblical evidence of the power of sin are not to be taken at face value because of new scientific insights, why should the call to liberation have any force for us today? Such reasoning is hollow. Christians may well call for the liberation of homosexuals from the cruel and unfair social and political conditions that contemporary social structures force them to endure, but this concern does not necessitate condoning or approving of homosexuality.

Analogy

Some argue using analogy to contend that Christians engaging in homosexual activities should be welcomed into the life of the church: As the Gentiles were accepted into the early church by Jewish Christians, so today homosexuals should be welcomed by heterosexual Christians. This analogy often moves from race or ethnicity to sexual practice, a dubious move. Those offering such arguments do not, of course, view the analogy this way; rather, they suggest that sexual orientation is a genetic condition or predisposition comparable to race, so that homosexuals do not simply act, but they "are." The science behind the assumptions of this reading of homosexuality is debated, and the argument is beyond resolution at the present.

Nevertheless, even if one grants the accuracy of this understanding of homosexuality, the argument breaks down at a number of points. First, at many places in the Old Testament the people of Israel looked forward to the inclusion of the Gentiles among God's kingdom; the prophets spoke of the inclusion of the Gentiles as an eschatological sign of God's triumph over evil. There is no Old Testament hope for the inclusion of homosexuals in the kingdom, nor is there a parallel New Testament hope for inclusion of practicing homosexuals in the church (e.g. Lev. 20:13; 1 Cor. 6:9–11). The biblical reading of homosexuality is consistent; the biblical portrait of the real position of Gentiles in God's kingdom is not—at one point the Gentiles are "out," but the dominant vision of the Bible looks forward to or records their being "in."

Another version of the argument by analogy ignores (even denies the validity of) the genetic factor of predisposition. Instead, the argument is that the early Jewish Christians accepted Gentiles into the church because of the undeniable presence of the Spirit in their lives. This is another form of the argument from experience that I considered above. To reiterate the central point: The manifestation of God's grace in conditions of human brokenness is the *good news* of the gospel! But grace occurring in brokenness does not endorse or vindicate the human condition of sin that grace seeks to redeem. Therefore, in either of its forms, the analogy to the inclusion of the Gentiles in the church has too many problems to be commended for serious consideration.

Conclusion Concerning Reason and Science

The data of science are not definitive. They describe in debated terms the ways things *are,* and they have no capacity to tell us how things *ought to be.* Operating with reason, which is almost always mixed with a heavy dose of emotion, we tend to think that the most appropriate course in relation to homosexuals is to offer them what is called "Christian love." Such love becomes functionally equivalent to "doing what seems nicest," which becomes the least awkward, least difficult, or least painful path of relations. Thus it may seem reasonable to offer homosexuals approval, rather than to relate to them in Christ's love, respect, compassion, concern, and care—that is, sharing freely in the truth of the gospel—while still disapproving of homosexual behavior. The call of Christ is to a direct and narrow life of faith, not to the wide and easy way of destruction. Simple acceptance, despite the best of intentions, may amount to cheap grace.

The combination of acceptance and disapproval in a relationship with compassion, concern, and care without condoning—this is the paradoxical pattern of life to which the Bible and the gospel call us. The challenge for Christians today is to learn to live in the light of God's simultaneous yes and no to all of humanity in Jesus Christ. To live in Christ's name means to commit ourselves to struggle with the ambiguities of life while seeking to be true to the gospel as we know it through the message of scripture. We

know Jesus Christ and God's will through the witness
of the Bible, so that while scripture is not the primary object of our devotion, it is the medium in which we encounter the message of God's gracious will for our lives.
Reason aids us in our attempt to comprehend the Bible,
but reason cannot replace the scriptures in a life of Christian devotion to God.

A Fresh Perspective
from the Teaching of Jesus

Through scripture we learn that homosexual behavior
is contrary to the will of God. Paul mentioned "the wrath
of God . . . revealed from heaven against all ungodliness
and wickedness of those who by their wickedness sup-
press the truth" prior to commenting on homosexual behavior in Romans 1. In the statement about homosexual
behavior per se, Paul remarked that persons committing
homosexual acts receive "in their own persons the due
penalty for their error." Elsewhere, however, the same Paul
declared about the experience of being a new creation in
Christ that God "reconciled us to himself through Christ
. . . that is, in Christ God was reconciling the world to himself, not counting their trespasses against them" (2 Cor.
5:18–19). Similarly, Jesus taught about divine judgment
and condemnation of the sinfulness of humanity (Matt.
11:32–42; 25:31–46) in the course of his ministry. In that
same ministry he called persons to him with the promise
of forgiveness (6:14) and rest (11:25–30), even declaring
that he died to secure a "covenant . . . for the forgiveness
of sins" (26:28).

For us the divine combination of judgment and grace,
of condemnation and forgiveness, of wrath and reconciliation are hard to fathom, and so we tend to eliminate one or

the other dimension of the paradox of God's relationship to humankind. We focus on judgment and wrath and contemplate damnation, or we savor reconciliation and grace and celebrate divine acceptance of sinful humanity. The tendency is to view God as a cosmic ogre, bound and determined to administer well-deserved punishment; or we envision God as an eternal Mr. Rogers, eager to welcome us all to the neighborhood of the kingdom. Wrath and reconciliation become theological oil and water, so that we opt for the ointment of righteous recompense or the refreshment of divine deliverance.

Jesus, however, lived with the dynamic tension of God's wrath and grace; in fact, he embodied the paradox. Jesus taught of the indisputable goodness of God, saying, "No one is good but God alone" (Luke 18:19). Indeed, he lived his life as an embodiment of divine good: "God anointed Jesus of Nazareth with the Holy Spirit and with power; . . . he went about doing good and healing all who were oppressed by the devil, for God was with him" (Acts 10:38). Yet Jesus taught of divine judgment, acted out God's judgment on the corruption of the Temple (Matt. 21:12–13), and pronounced a curse on the fruitless fig tree (Matt. 21:18–22).

How, then, are we to understand God's disposition toward homosexual behavior? Do we opt for wrath or grace? Or is there an intermediate understanding?

In the course of the Sermon of the Mount, Matthew records Jesus' saying:

> Is there anyone among you who, if your child asks for bread, will give a stone? Or if the child asks for a fish, will give a snake? If you then, who are evil, know how to give good gifts to your children, how much more will your Father in heaven give good things to those who ask him! (Matt. 7:9–11).

Luke presents the same material in the context of Jesus' journey to Jerusalem:

> Is there anyone among you who, if your child asks for a fish, will give a snake instead of a fish? Or if the child asks for an egg, will give a scorpion? If you then, who are evil, know how to give good gifts to your children, how much more will the heavenly Father give the Holy Spirit to those who ask him! (Luke 11:11–13).

If we reflect theologically about God's relationship to homosexual persons by analogy to human parenting—particularly the response of human parents to their own children who are homosexuals—we may gain clarity about God's regard for homosexual persons.

When sons and daughters inform their parents that they are homosexuals, the parents react in three basic ways. First, some parents, because the child is their own flesh and blood, immediately accept the news and become ardent defenders of their child's sexual behavior. (The same reaction occurs with parents of heterosexuals who defend the premarital or extramarital activities of their children.) This reaction is all "grace" with no judgment, and no reconciliation is needed. Second, on the opposite extreme, some parents simply and immediately disavow their homosexual children because their sexual behavior is completely unacceptable to them. (Again, parents of heterosexuals can have the same reaction when their children engage in sexual activities that are deemed inappropriate.) Here the reaction is all "judgment" with no grace, and no reconciliation is possible. Third, there are parents who neither immediately accept nor reject their homosexual children. Rather, these parents struggle with the sexual activity of their sons and daughters. They cannot and do not approve of such sexual behavior. Yet they continue to love them in spite of their sexual activity. (Once again, the parallel to parents of heterosexuals should be clear.) Here, at last, we find judgment, grace, and a genuine yearning for reconciliation in the rich theological mix that suggests we are close to the image of God that we seek for forming and directing our own relationships to persons who are homosexuals.

Given the evidence of scripture—that God is love and that homosexual behavior is contrary to God's will—I believe that God is like the loving human parents who hear the news of their children's homosexuality, and despite their complete disapproval of such sexual activities, nevertheless love their children with all their hearts while continuing to disapprove completely of their homosexuality. If God is like these parents, then we can make sense of the Bible's simultaneous or paradoxical images of God as both the God of wrath and the God of grace.

Jesus Christ as
Personal Hermeneutic

The personal encounter with Jesus Christ as the embodiment of God's holiness brings a realistic assessment of life to humanity. When Simon Peter met Jesus by the Lake of Gennesaret and experienced God's astonishing power at work in him (Luke 5:1–11), Simon fell down before Jesus and cried out, "Go away from me, Lord, for I am a sinful man!" In his personal engagement with humans, Jesus Christ brings the discerning light of God's holiness to bear on human existence, so that sinfulness is made apparent. The illuminating encounter with the person of Jesus Christ, however, does not bring a recognition of sinfulness that paralyzes. Simon Peter saw his sin and confessed his sinfulness, but Jesus did not dwell upon Simon's confession;

rather, he issued a call to a transformed life of service that liberated Simon from his sinfulness.

A personal encounter with Jesus Christ does not simply bring a comforting affirmation of who we are, for the presence of Jesus Christ in our lives confronts us with God's holiness and moves us to a candid confession of our sinfulness. Yet admitting our sin we know no condemnation, for the personal encounter with Jesus Christ redeems us from our sin as he sets us on a new course of living. Sin is acknowledged, but sin is set aside. New life dawns as we meet Jesus Christ face to face and then admit that we have failed to do God's will; in turn, we experience forgiveness as we hear Christ's call to a new life.

This paradigm of personal encounter with Jesus Christ has meaning for every human life. None of us is so pure as to escape the scrutiny of God's holiness in Jesus Christ, but none of us is so great a sinner as to be beyond the power of God's redemption. Jesus Christ comes to us, and when we see him for who he is, then we know who we are. In honest confession, through the call of Jesus Christ, we experience forgiveness and the transformation of our lives. This is the gospel for all humanity: the truth of God's holiness revealed in Jesus Christ, the recognition of our sinfulness, the forgiveness of our sins, and the reconciliation through Christ of our lives to the God who loves us and seeks our redemption.

4. Conclusions

Many elements of the reflections that have gone in the chapters before need summarizing here. The role of the Bible in the life of the church (at least in the Reformed tradition), and the crucial Christian combination of candor and compassion are matters that merit repeated reflection. In turn, the implications of this study—what are Christians to think and do about homosexuals, about church membership for homosexuals, and about ordination for homosexuals—needs commentary and elaboration. Finally, some vital matters of basic Christian life require comment.

Affirmation of Biblical Authority

The Reformed tradition is defined by its clear affirmation of biblical authority. Members of the Presbyterian Church (U.S.A.) confess that "the Scriptures are not a witness among others, but the witness without parallel" (The Confession of 1967, 9.27). Because "we trust in God the Holy Spirit . . . who . . . rules our faith and life in Christ through Scriptures" (A Brief Statement of Faith, 10.4), we seek as faithful stewards of God's grace to live our lives in a vigorous relationship to the Bible. We trust that in and through the Bible God speaks to us, and through our concern with scripture, guided by the Holy Spirit, we find and do God's will. Increasingly, however, persons who have religious or social sensibilities that lead them to advocate accepting homosexual behavior simply dismiss the normative role of scripture in Christian life. One hears today that *sola scriptura* (the Reformation's emphasis on "scripture alone" over against human experience or tradition as the authoritative guide to faith) is an outmoded concept, an idea beyond its time, with little or no value for life in the late twentieth century. In part, people take this position because they react to the all-too-real abuses of the authority of scripture. They have heard the phrase "the Bible says" used as a cudgel in such outrageous ways that they come to blame the Bible for its misuse by mean-spirited interpreters. The abuse of the Bible is no reason, however, to discard the scriptures as the norm of Christian life. The authority of scripture functions poorly as a club, for the Bible's authority is more that of testimony to revelation requiring reasoning than that of received regulations requiring compliance. The Bible gives us "the whole counsel of God . . . unto which nothing at any time is to be added" (The Westminster Confession of Faith, 6.006). This conviction does not seek to restrict the innovative work of God's Spirit, but it expresses the security of the believers that the Spirit does not contradict the voice of God as spoken in earlier times of God's involvement with humanity.

Some persons who do not reject the authority of the scriptures still seek to redefine their plain sense in relation to matters that are controversial in contemporary society. Yet when we call the scriptures "the Supreme Judge, by which all controversies of religion are to be determined" (The Westminster Confession of Faith, 6.010), we name the Bible as an enduring witness on issues of faith and practice. Thus when the Bible speaks clearly—despite the obfuscation projected on it by revisionist interpreters—we are called to listen as we seek to be faithful in the understanding of faithfulness found in the Reformed tradition. When the Bible speaks clearly—despite the objections of those offended by biblical morality who would stand above the scriptures in judgment and who seek to countermand the plain sense of the texts—we are called to take the message of the Bible to heart as if it were the word of a devoted friend, faithfully seeking our best interest, honest, incisive, but at times less than fully pleasant to hear. Yet some current critics of the scriptures seek to tame the written word of God, to make it immediately soothing, or at least therapeutic, to modern ears.

"I recognize the authority of the Bible, except in instances when it would inhibit natural human development," boasts one critic. Yet such recognition is *no* recognition. Affirming the authority of scripture does not mean unplugging the mind and following the rules; rather, recognizing the authority of scripture means that we do not pick the parts that please us and ignore—or, perhaps worse, imaginatively remake—the sections that we find difficult or unacceptable. Scripture has its own integrity that is to be honored. The critic who reads the Bible and rejects its teaching—its view of God, the world, and human existence in the world in relation to God—is a better friend of those who seek to recognize the authority of Scripture than are those false friends who claim to love the Bible but who labor assiduously to redefine its perspectives.

The Bible and the Life of the Church

Biblical authority is not biblical tyranny: We read, reflect, evaluate, reevaluate, respond, react, and reconcile ourselves with scripture; but we never simply remake or reject it—if we affirm its authority. Our encounter with the Bible is with the canon of scripture. We do not live by a verse, a chapter, or even by a book (although we all tend to have a "canon within the canon"). We focus and live in relation to *all* of scripture, struggling to make sense of the complexity of life by connecting it with the complexity of canon. The scriptures mediate Christ and his message to us. We listen for a biblical word, knowing that scriptural perspectives exist and that we are able confidently to think and to decide about matters of living in relation to Christ's word in the scriptures. When the Bible speaks in a single voice, however, the ultimate decision we make is for or against the scriptures with the full awareness that a choice against the Bible means that we claim an authority higher than "the witness without parallel."

The Reformed tradition lives by the authority of scripture. We feed on the nourishment of the Bible, seeking and trusting its message as God's word written for our attention, reflection, direction, and edification. While the Bible is not a rule book—meaning a book of rules to be followed mindlessly—the Bible is a book that has authority to serve as God's medium for communication through the Holy Spirit, who "rules our faith and life in Christ through Scripture."

One cannot "sell" the notion of the authority of the Bible. The Holy Spirit either persuades persons of the crucial place and function of the scriptures for Christian life, or not. The authority of scripture is not a debatable or marginal or redefinable tenet of the Reformed tradition. Thus the burden of proof for making a case for an exceptional view—such as the idea of the validity of homosexual behavior for members of the church—belongs to those who would argue against scripture; it is not the task of those who hold to the plain, univocal sense of the biblical texts to establish the acceptability of their understanding of the inappropriateness of homosexual behavior.

Candor and Compassion

An awareness of the biblical perspective on homosexual activity might seem to have no relevance for most church members who are neither themselves homosexuals nor involved knowingly with others who are homosexuals. But today, given that this particular subject is a lively topic of discussion and debate in the life of the church, members of congregations cannot simply ignore the conversation. Rather, when we hear and heed the biblical disapproval of homosexual behavior, the message has meaning for all our lives. This observation is not a suggestion that the scriptures foster the exposure of homosexual activities, but the decision one makes about the validity of homosexual behavior for members of the Christian community is effectively a decision about the authority of the Bible in the life of the church. What, then, in today's context, does an affirmation of the authority of the Bible mean that we say or do?

Christians who affirm biblical authority are called to a combination of candor and compassion concerning the issue of homosexuality—a blend of ingredients that should, indeed, characterize Christian thought and life at every level. In candor, from a careful study of and reflection on the scriptures, and with a full measure of humility because we recognize and confess our own sinfulness, we can say that we cannot and do not condone homosexual activity as sexual practice in accordance with the intention of God for humanity. Indeed, because of our confidence in scripture and the guidance of the Holy Spirit, we disagree with those who voice and seek approval for homosexual activity.

When we voice such thinking, however, we should re-
alize that the love of God for all of sinful humanity
requires us to be concerned for the very persons whose
sexual behavior we reject. (The same could be said about
the sinful behavior of an adulterer—a less controversial
issue at present, but a topic that could be treated similarly.)
In a society such as ours, persons of Christian commitments should be concerned about the unjust and inhu-
mane treatment that is regularly visited upon
homosexuals. Both gay bashing and the efforts to deny
basic civil rights to homosexuals are activities contrary to
the kind of compassion, concern, and love revealed by
God in Jesus Christ. One can propose all kinds of "what-if"
scenarios to think about homosexuality as a social issue,
and one can imagine a variety of "Christian reactions" to
particular situations involving homosexuals; but no action
or reaction can properly be called Christian that is not
characterized by the kind of love God manifests in Christ:

> Love is patient; love is kind; love is not envious or boast-
> ful or arrogant or rude. It does not insist on its own way;
> it is not irritable or resentful; it does not rejoice in
> wrongdoing, but rejoices in the truth. It bears all things,
> believes all things, hopes all things, endures all things
> (1 Cor. 13:4–7).

Christians committed to biblical authority are not necessarily compelled to a special recognition of homosexuals
or to the granting of special status to such persons as a social class or minority group, but Christians are compelled
by the gospel to view all humans as children of God, sinners of different kinds, all of whom are worthy of decent
and fair treatment—even if we disagree with some over
the appropriateness of their sexual behavior. The Bible and
Christian tradition consistently view adultery as sinful be-

havior that is comparable to homosexuality in its severity and unacceptability. Yet few if any today are concerned and at work to restrict the rights of adulterers, as are some opponents of homosexuality, who busily seek to place social and political restrictions on homosexuals. Adulterers are not commonly singled out for special showings of social disdain, despite religious denunciation of adultery.

A blend of Christian compassion and candor may lead us to voice disapproval of both homosexuality and adultery, but we must always remember that God extends forgiveness to humanity in Jesus Christ and calls sinners to be reconciled. As we speak against particular sinful behavior, we relate to others—especially those whom we oppose—as ambassadors for Christ, so that we tell them of the love of God and call them to the freedom of reconciliation. We may never voice disagreement or disapproval of homosexuality without speaking and living out the even more compelling word of God's grace in Jesus Christ.

Church Membership for Homosexuals

If the Bible regards homosexual behavior as sinful activity, what does that imply about church membership for homosexuals? The church is the body of believers who confess themselves to be forgiven and saved through God's grace at work in Jesus Christ. All members of the church are sinners, grateful for forgiveness and seeking to grow in grace. Every church member claims the reality of divine forgiveness, but every church member still experiences the influence of the real power of sin in life. No Christian is perfect.

The doors of the church stand open to all who confess their allegiance to Jesus Christ. Many of the arguments from experience for the approval of homosexuality cite the

clear, real evidences of God's grace in the lives of homosexuals. While such arguments do not prove the appropriateness of homosexual behavior, they do testify to the
reality of grace in particular human lives. One heterosexual Christian has said, "When I confessed Jesus Christ as
Lord and Savior, I began to find him at work in my life saving me from things I didn't know were sinful and from
which I didn't know I needed saving." Perfection is not a
prerequisite for a genuine confession of faith in Christ.

While the church cannot offer approval of homosexual
activity, the church can also not deny the validity of faith
in less-than-perfect humans. If approval of one's homosexual behavior becomes a condition for one's joining the
church, then the church faces an insurmountable problem;
for Christians seeking to recognize and to honor the authority of the Bible will insist that no such approval is possible. If there is no demand for approval of homosexual
activity, there is no reason to deny church membership
to the homosexual who takes her or his place along with
other forgiven sinners in the corporate body of Christ.

Unfortunately, to some people this observation sounds
like the now notorious policy of the United States military
services, "Don't ask; don't tell." In fact, however, the logic
is not the same. The military has attempted to exclude homosexual persons from military service, a policy allowing majority prejudice or opinion to set the standards of inclusion
and exclusion. The church seeks to include all sinners who
profess faith in Jesus Christ as Lord and Savior, a practice
that means "whosoever will may come." The concern of
the church is with a person's faith in Jesus Christ, not with
sexuality. Nevertheless, the desire to win approval of what
scripture considers sinful activity as a condition of church
membership introduces an element that itself—whether
concerning homosexual or some other behavior—is inap-

propriate and inadmissible as a condition of membership in the church.

This issue will be an ongoing matter for the church to discuss. Nevertheless, as the report "The Church and Homosexuality" (1978) of The United Presbyterian Church in the United States of America states,

> As persons repent and believe, they become members of Christ's body. The church is not a citadel of the morally perfect; it is a hospital for sinners. It is the fellowship where contrite, needy people rest their hope for salvation on Christ and his righteousness. Here in community they seek and receive forgiveness and new life. The church must become the nurturing community so that all whose lives come short of the glory of God are converted, reoriented, and built up into Christian community. It may be only in the context of loving community, appreciation, pastoral care, forgiveness, and nurture that homosexual persons can come to a clear understanding of God's pattern for their sexual expression.
>
> There is room in the church for all who give honest affirmation to the vows required for membership in the church. Homosexual persons who sincerely affirm "Jesus Christ is my Lord and Savior" and "I intend to be his disciple, to obey his word, and to show his love" should not be excluded from membership ("The Church and Homosexuality," The United Presbyterian Church in the United States of America [New York: Office of the General Assembly, 1978], 59).

Nothing found in the course of the present study would advocate altering this approach to the question of church membership for homosexuals. In fact, the biblical materials examined themselves show the correctness of this position, and they mitigate the harsh elements of tradition that would maintain that church membership for homosexuals is inappropriate or impossible.

Ordination for Homosexuals

The case for church membership for homosexuals should not, however, be extended logically to argue for the ordination of persons engaging in homosexual activities. Ordained persons are not an elite, but they serve a particular role in the life of the church. With regard to ordination for church office, the *Book of Order* of the Presbyterian Church (U.S.A.) states the following:

> The persons elected by the church to service in the offices of the church . . . shall be ordained to these offices by the church. Ordination is the act by which the church sets apart persons to be presbyters (ministers of the Word and Sacrament or elders) or deacons (*Book of Order*, G-14.0101).

At the service of ordination and installation of officers of the church, the *Book of Order* gives the following among the guidelines:

> The minister shall ask those preparing to be ordained or installed to stand before the congregation and to answer the following questions:
>
> a. Do you trust in Jesus Christ your Savior, acknowledge him Lord of all and Head of the church, and through him believe in one God, Father, Son, and Holy Spirit?
>
> b. Do you accept the Scriptures of the Old and New Testaments to be, by the Holy Spirit, the unique and authoritative witness to Jesus Christ in the church universal, and God's Word to you?
>
> c. Do you sincerely receive and adopt the essential tenets of the Reformed faith as expressed in the confessions of our church as authentic and reliable expositions of what Scripture leads us to believe and do, and will you be instructed and led by those confessions as you lead the people of God?

d. Will you fulfill your office in obedience to Jesus Christ, under the authority of Scripture, and be continually guided by our confessions? (*Book of Order*, G-14.0207).

Six other related questions or sets of questions fill out the constitutional questions that are asked of future officers at the service of ordination and installation, but these four questions inquire about the essential matters that form the faith and focus of candidates for ordination. In evaluating the question of the possibility of ordination of homosexuals, the members of the Task Force to Study Homosexuality wrote in their background paper, "The Church and Homosexuality," which was received by the 190th General Assembly of The United Presbyterian Church in the United States of America, the following statement:

> To be an ordained officer is to be a human instrument, touched by divine powers but still an earthen vessel. As portrayed in Scripture, the officers set before the church and community an example of piety, love, service, and moral integrity. Officers are not free from repeated expressions of sin. Neither are members and officers free to adopt a lifestyle of conscious, continuing, and unresisted sin in any area of their lives. For the church to ordain a self-affirming, practicing homosexual person to ministry would be to act in contradiction to its charter and calling in Scripture, setting in motion both within the church and society serious contradictions to the will of Christ.
>
> The repentant homosexual person who finds the power of Christ redirecting his or her sexual desires toward a married heterosexual commitment, or finds God's power to control his or her desires and to adopt a celibate lifestyle, can certainly be ordained, all other qualifications being met. Indeed, such candidates must be welcomed and be free to share their full identity.

> Their experience of hatred and rejection may have given
> them a unique capacity for love and sensitivity as
> wounded healers among heterosexual Christians, and
> they may be incomparably equipped to extend the
> church's outreach to the homosexual community.
>
> We believe that Jesus Christ intends the ordination of
> officers to be a sign of hope to the church and to the
> world. Therefore our present understanding of God's
> will precludes the ordination of persons who do not re-
> pent of homosexual practice ("The Church and Homo-
> sexuality," The United Presbyterian Church in the
> United States of America [New York: Office of the Gen-
> eral Assembly, 1978], 60).

These paragraphs are the subject of ongoing debate, despite a clear majority of the members of the Presbyterian
Church (U.S.A.) being in agreement with the statement.
The matter of the authority of scripture is at the heart of
the issue of ordination and at the center of this particular
controversy over the ordination of homosexuals. At present, without simply ignoring or abandoning belief in and
commitment to the authority of scripture to lead us to believe and do God's will, we have no evidence to direct us
to an understanding and a practice different from that presented to the church in 1978.

The biblical assessment of homosexual behavior artic-
ulates a condemnation of such activity. The conditions for
ordination in the *Book of Order* rightly recognize the authoritative place of the scriptures in the life of the church,
particularly in guiding the lives and work of ordained
ministers. The affirmation of the Bible as being authoritative precludes the church's giving either explicit or tacit
approval to homosexual practices through the ordination
of persons who, in a self-affirming manner, engage in
homosexual acts.

The Gospel and Sexuality

The subject of homosexuality is only one part of the larger topic of human sexuality that now regularly exercises the church. Most matters that fall under the umbrella of human sexuality become problems in contemporary discussion, so that homosexuality is no different from any other topic related to sex. Even—perhaps especially—in discussions in the church, we become embroiled in controversy over sexuality. This happens primarily because there is little or no theology in the conversation. Our talk leaps to issues such as "rights and responsibilities" and "oppression and liberation." We quickly and easily focus on ourselves as if we were hermetically sealed individuals or groups who require only understanding and acceptance from others for life to be good. We get our discussions off on the wrong foot, however, by focusing on ourselves. Therefore, when God and God's will finally come into the conversation about matters of sexuality there is little to imagine that God can do other than offer approval of who we say we are and have the right to be. We assume we discern the truth about ourselves with a clarity that should inform both other humans and God, denying that we may be blinded by the power of sin. Yet, despite much current discussion, God the Great Approver of all humanity is not much of a God at all. Rather than viewing God as the sovereign creator of all creation, our assumptions cast God as one who endorses our every whim without criticism.

Paul faced a similar situation in relation to the Christians in Corinth, where members of the church had decided and declared that "All things are lawful for me!" In reasoning with the Corinthian Christians Paul used a pattern of rhetoric in which he quoted the position of the

Corinthians. He created an imaginary dialogue in order to respond to their thinking. The conversation goes back and forth:

> CORINTHIANS: All things are lawful for me;
> PAUL: but not all things are beneficial.
> CORINTHIANS: All things are lawful for me;
> PAUL: but I will not be dominated by anything.
> CORINTHIANS: Food is meant for the stomach and the stomach for food;
> PAUL: and God will destroy both one and the other.

The slogan of the Corinthians says literally, "All things [are] to me permissible." They could have learned this statement from Paul himself, for he never denied its validity; rather, he explained the real sense of such an idea. The Corinthians took the notion of their freedom in Christ and made all kinds of claims about what they might do with their lives. For those in Corinth, Christian freedom was an abstraction that gave license to their desires and actions. Paul responded by particularizing the concept of Christian liberty. Freedom, according to Paul, is characterized by pursuing what is best; freedom does not lead to a new form of slavery. The Corinthians mistakenly claimed an inner freedom that placed them above matters of everyday living, and they were eager to demonstrate their liberation from the mundane.

The will to display freedom had apparently gotten out of hand. Some of the Corinthians assumed that their freedom in Christ meant they could gratify their every appetite. Paul expressed shock that some had concluded from the idea that all foods are fit for consumption that they were at liberty to engage in casual sex with prostitutes in celebration of their freedom.

Paul's critique called the Corinthians into a responsible relationship to "the Lord." Freedom, Paul told the Corinthians, is "for the Lord," not merely for personal pleasure. To make his point with all possible force, Paul quoted Gen. 2:24 in 1 Cor. 6:16b. On the one hand, he used scripture to denounce involvement with prostitutes; on the other hand, the citation led to a crucial statement of the nature of the spiritual union of Christians with the Lord.

In v. 18–20 Paul's rhetoric takes the form of a clear frontal attack. He directed the Corinthians to "shun fornication!" Then he informed them that their "body" is "a temple of the Holy Spirit within [them]." Paul bluntly told the Corinthians, "You are not your own." Why? Because as Paul reminded them, they were bought with a price. That the Corinthians belonged to God was the ultimate qualification of their freedom.

Throughout this section Paul jabbed at his readers with the rhetorical refrain, "Do you not know. . . ?" The implication was that the Corinthians did not know what they should have known. Today the situation is often the same.

The truth of the gospel is that our bodies are not ours to do with whatever we want or will to do. Our world teaches us not to like this message. Yet we are creatures, part of God's creation. God is the creator, and in giving us the good gift of life God created us for a purpose—or better, we were created (we did not create ourselves) for God's own purposes. Our bodies are not ours alone, for by God's grace they are the temple of the Holy Spirit. No matter what we think or claim for ourselves, God is our sovereign Lord. Thus the freedom to which the gospel calls is the responsible living of our lives as faithful creatures who are obedient to God's will.

What we do with our lives matters. God cares how we live. In faith we believe that because God is good and that because God loves us, God gave us Jesus Christ, the scriptures, and the Holy Spirit to guide us in the living of our God-given days. What then do we say? Thanks be to God for the good gifts of grace!